JR LITTLE

LISTENING BRANDS

HOW DATA IS REWRITING THE RULES OF BRANDING

LISTENING BRANDS

How Data Is Rewriting the Rules of Branding

ISBN 978-1-61961-364-5

LIONCREST

PUBLISHING

The views expressed in this book are my own and are not representative of the views of my employer.

I would like to thank Garland, Joshua, Diego, Adrian, Carl, Doug, Sanjay, Delphine, Cate, Ashley, Gina, Duncan, Sharon, and Dan.

CONTENTS

Introduction: The Value of Listening to the Unspoken 9

PART ONE: IDENTIFYING THE PROBLEM

1. Who is Holding the Megaphone? 27
2. What To Do First? Be Curious 41
3. What Kind of Listening Are You Doing? 55
4. Back to Brand Building, Circa 2007 67

PART TWO: GATHERING DATA

5. What Does "Data" Mean Today, Anyway? 81
6. A New Vocabulary for Listening 97
7. Change...or Else 105
8. Listening Technology and Listening Teams 117
9. Analog Lifestyle Data vs. Digital Data 131
10. Let's Get Social 147

PART THREE: ACTING ON THE DATA

11. How Data Can Be Used to Build Micro Teams 163
12. Lessons from Real Brands 175
13. How Data Can Be Used to Refine Message,
    Product and Context 183
14. How to Avoid Being a Dinosaur 197

Conclusion: The Future of Listening to Data 207
About the Author 215

THE VALUE OF LISTENING TO THE UNSPOKEN

My ability to listen to people and keenly observe human behavior developed early.

It wasn't a matter of choice. It was a matter of survival.

As a child, I learned quickly that I needed to be a chameleon. I had to adapt to any situation that presented itself. It was essential that I pay attention, take in my surroundings and measure people's moods and personalities.

I grew up in an evangelical Christian family, on a farm in North Carolina. If you don't know much about North Carolina, it's pretty much the heartland of very conservative social values in the United States. It was where "televange-lists" were born: Billy Graham and his son were from there,

Jerry Falwell was just a couple of hours north, and remember Jim and Tammy Faye Bakker? If not, do a quick search of Tammy Faye—she was quite a character.

So I grew up on a farm, in an extremely socially conservative environment.

And I'm gay.

What you're probably picturing right now—a small, shy "country boy" trying to fit into a community where he didn't feel he truly belonged—was my reality.

It was beautiful in North Carolina, no doubt about that. It still is: open space, clean air and green vistas spiced with the intoxicating aroma of pine, oak and maple trees.

But that idyllic picture ended there, at least for me.

Business is Personal—Family Dynamics

Growing up, I was part of a big, loud and opinionated family, all of us living in several houses set scattered between barns and silos on 2,000 acres of farmland. Farming was not a hobby for us. This was a serious business. It was our livelihood, and we were all part of it—every single family member, no matter their age. We grew corn, wheat and soybeans, and we raised chickens for Tyson Corporation. We had horses and greenhouses, and each segment of the family farmed what they wanted to on their own patch of land. My mother ran the greenhouses, my brother the crops and chickens, and my sister the horses. And me? Well, I just pitched in. I didn't really have passion for any of it. I wanted to draw, dress up and dance!

"Hang on, JR," you might be saying right now. "This doesn't sound like a marketing book. What does all this have to do with becoming a 'listening brand'?"

The answer will become clearer as you read through this book. But even if you read nothing more than this introduction, you'll understand the basis of what it means to be a brand that listens.

Business is always personal. We are—inside and outside of our work—reflections of our life experiences. And these events shape the way we think and behave.

My life story goes a long way toward explaining why I do what I do as a professional—and even more importantly, why and how I can help you by sharing what's in this book. Because in many ways, my childhood, in particular, demonstrates exactly what brands must do if they're going to adapt to the fast-changing communications environment that has developed over the past few years. I will argue that the adaptation needed now is the greatest paradigm shift in the history of the communications industry.

As a child in a conservative, religious, work-around-the-clock world, and knowing I was different from everyone else, I had no choice but to learn how to interpret and relate to whatever was happening in the moment.

I learned how to read people and how to understand their motives. I perfected the art of picking up on people's cues and assessing quickly if someone was a kind person (or not). For the most part, I avoided bullying and fit in just fine because I was an excellent listener.

Looking back, I can see that honing these skills kept me from being in uncomfortable situations—or even in physical or emotional danger. The family relationships I witnessed were often strained. Really, the only thing we all had in common was a commitment to making the farm succeed and putting food on the table. As a result, I was often seeing through someone's exterior and into their motivations. When you combine astute listening and observing skills with an evangelical, spiritual upbringing, you get someone who can relate to other people and understand their struggles. A bit deep for a kid, but anyone who has felt like an outsider, a minority, can likely relate.

That's who I was as a child.

That is still who I am today.

And that is why I love my work.

In my boisterous family, my older brother and sister were—and still are—outspoken and charismatic alpha personalities. There was a great sense of pride in my immediate and extended family about how hard everyone worked and how athletic and outgoing they all were.

I, on the other hand, was the introverted one. I honestly

don't know if the introversion came first, or if it came after becoming aware that I was gay. I was also the creative one, the smart one, the puny one, the weak one. While I'm not puny or weak anymore, I'm still a more introverted person. Over time, I've learned to be comfortable being on a stage or speaking in front of large crowds. Stay tuned for a story related to that in a moment.

My natural instinct is to stay quiet...and listen.

That skill has served me—and my clients—very well in the years since. My childhood experiences and, later, my education, brought me to an understanding of human behavior that has allowed me to help my clients serve their customers more effectively, not to mention more profitably.

How, exactly?

When you realize at an early age that you're a little bit different, you try to figure out why. You quickly try to understand why you think the way you think, and why other people think and behave the way they do. I look back now and realize I was almost like a psychologist or anthropologist, experimenting and forming my own hypotheses, trying to make sense of everything and trying to understand the motivations behind the differences.

Are you starting to see how my story relates to the topic of this book?

The family dynamic became even more complex when I was eight years old, and my father passed away from a heart attack; we worked very hard on the farm and loved deep fried Southern food. I became very close to my grandfather after my father's death. He taught me a lot—everything I know, really—about business. He had dropped out of school when he was about eight years old, so to him, I was an adult.

A veteran of World War II, my grandfather built the farm from nothing, and he raised me almost like a Baby Boomer would have been raised: with that kind of work ethic and structure. From my earliest memories, my grandfather got me involved with the business of the farm. I was handling farm equipment and even driving trucks on the road by age 12. My grandfather didn't seem to see me as a child, and he didn't treat me that way.

As a result, my childhood was devoted to learning the family farming business, led by my grandfather's teaching. Alongside my inner life of anticipating and reacting to other people's behavior, I saw that the farm had to adapt and adjust as market demand shifted. There was fluctuation from one season to the next; sometimes everything had to shift in response to market and weather changes. Maybe corn was selling better, or wheat was selling better, or maybe we had a drought in one season—or worse, a hurricane—so we had to overproduce in the next season to make up for the losses.

My grandfather was always focused on work, and I acted like his assistant. I would ride around with him in his truck and check on the crops and livestock. But observant young me was also paying attention to my mother. She loved gardening and flowers, so I would help her in the greenhouses and gardens. I also used my creative juices to help her in the flowerbeds and make arrangements for the church altar. I was her assistant, too. This pattern of assisting—helping—went on with every member of my family. (Did I mention I was the youngest in a large family?)

I was jumping in and out of different roles all the time. At some point along the way, I realized that if I wanted to build relationships with people, I had to do the things they wanted to do—join them in activities that they enjoyed. I had to be a helpful presence.

A Different Goal for Business

Let's be clear about something here. This book is about new ways of listening to customers and prospects, about tuning into their wants and needs and responding quickly. Outside the context of this book—such as my situation as a child—this kind of activity might be seen as rather sad. I was looking for acceptance and doing whatever I could to get it. That was my childhood reality.

In business, the end goal is slightly different. It's acceptance and connection, yes, but it's also a transaction. The underlying principle, however, is the same: observe, listen, respond accordingly and build a connection. One of the things I learned in studying human behavior is that everyone is trying to get a need met, in every relationship. In this way, work life and home life are very similar.

Today, I can look back to my childhood and draw distinct parallels with what I see now in communications. The approach companies use in talking to people must adapt and adjust as consumers and culture change.

I eventually left the family farm and graduated from university, where I studied human development (surprise, surprise). At that time, I was still trying to uncover my identity and wrestling with my sexuality, and I was really interested in the science of understanding people. But when I went to a graduate program to become a marriage and family therapist, I knew immediately that it wasn't the right path for me. I spent some time working for nonprofit organizations, deepening my compassion and my listening skills, but social services still didn't seem like a good "fit."

In my college years, I was also interested in design and the arts. It wasn't the artistic element that captivated me as much as the psychology behind design: learning how to persuade an audience with imagery and words. That's a good thing, too, because my artistic and design skills were missing the mark, and I knew that traditional design wasn't the right path for me, either.

When I took a course in branding in New York, led by a professor from one of the big branding agencies, I fell in love with the idea that human insight could help to create persuasive communication. The professor would give us problems to solve through words and images: problems with society, problems with businesses. I really enjoyed the process of ideation and creative thinking, what some people would call "strategy." I was less enamored with asking questions like, "What's the right color? What's the right shape?" It wasn't the basics of design that I liked, but the thinking behind the design. That love of creative strategy inspired me to study strategic communications at Columbia University in New York.

Finally, I felt like I had landed on something that connected all the dots of my life.

A Career in Branding is Launched

I first started working at a branding agency after a three-year stint in advertising. In all of those agencies, we operated in the same traditional way. We had huge retainer contracts with big companies, like the largest bank in the world or what was, at the time, the largest tech company in the world. We would consult with them and suggest rather vaguely, "Oh, your personality should be this way," or "Your tone should be like this," or "You should use this messaging," or "This should be your visual communication style." We told them that if they were consistent, if they just kept driving the same message home over and over again, that eventually they would sway people to love them—because this is what had always worked.

I soared in this work. It came easy to me. And I was having a blast. To me, working long hours thinking creatively, sharing my opinions and traveling the world was a hell of a lot better than shoveling cow manure. I felt like I had found my life's calling.

But then I started to sense that what I was great at doing was starting to matter less; something was changing in the world of advertising, marketing and communications. Over the six years that I was in that branding agency, which included the recession in 2008-2010, things started to shift, and fast. It was almost like a perfect storm. We had a tipping point with the recession, where people were not trusting businesses, especially in the West. People were angry at corporate society and at banks and financial institutions, in particular. Remember Lehman Brothers? At the same time, social media platforms like Facebook and Twitter were really taking off and gaining mass appeal and usage.

As a result, everything was shaken up in terms of advertising and marketing, not to mention economically and socially around the world. Suddenly, the people with the voice were actually the people themselves. A brand's message could be obliterated by something going viral on social media.

One of the earliest examples I can remember was BP, British Petroleum. BP had branded itself using the traditional methods to look like an environment-loving company, with a beautiful green-and-gold logo that resembled a flower.

Then in 2010, the BP oil spill disaster happened in the Gulf of Mexico. In a live broadcast, you had a camera focused on the oil spewing into the water. At the same time, you had social media messages bombarding the Internet: thousands and thousands of public-generated comments against BP. That was one of the first big cases that I remember where it became clear to me that the voice of the people on social media was stronger than the voice of the corporation.

We saw what happened in Egypt in 2011, too, where social

media was a huge force for social change. This type of social media impact started happening even in places around the world once considered remote. Good Internet speeds, mobile devices and proliferating social media platforms have allowed the people to grab the power of their voice back from corporate and even political power.

Things are Still Changing

Some of the puzzle pieces are still coming together on all of this, and the picture is not yet clear.

What I know with certainty, though, is that the role of the brand today is to listen—and to be helpful to the consumer based on what the people are doing and saying online.

This core idea is not too far off from the basic principles of branding, meaning to differentiate and find a way to stand out. Unfortunately, the old branding methodology dictated that the way to differentiate yourself was simply to say something different.

Saying something over and over again, no matter how different it is from what your competitors are saying or how loudly you're saying it, doesn't work anymore. Now, to differentiate means that you are being helpful in a unique—and better—way than other brands, inside and even outside of your category.

There really is something exciting in the air, where businesses are succeeding not because of the strength of their overarching brand, but because of their intelligent use of digital and social data.

What You'll Learn in this Book

This book will give you an idea of what's happening now—and potentially in the future—in the digital space: how we can listen to, learn from and act upon all the data that's being produced.

It's really designed to help anyone who is working in the area of brand building and/or marketing, whether you're in a company or an agency, or even if you're an entrepreneur. The reader need not be the person responsible for the nuts and bolts of data management. This book is more about the bigger implications and the impact data will have on everyone's job. Having said that, my hope is that you will feel less intimated by data at the end and that you will feel validated in your preexisting knowledge. But don't expect this book to solve all your problems. As we say in the South, there is more than one way to skin a cat. I'm still not sure why we say that, but the point is, other people will have different approaches, and the digital world moves fast—very fast. Over the course of just a few weeks, I have had to tweak this book to stay up to date. So alas, this book is a look at where we are heading, not an end solution.

We'll look at some corporate examples later on in this book, but here is a personal story of listening that you may relate to. It's an example from the non-digital world that illustrates what we can—and should—do in the digital world.

You're going to a conference, and you're trying to network with other people: maybe looking for someone who could be useful for your business, someone who could join your team or even a future employer. The best way to do that is to listen, so you can determine which people have similar interests, vision and goals. Then you can make an educated guess about what their needs are, because if you can relate your need to their need, you're more likely to get the solution you want. This is the trick to interviews, as well.

But oftentimes, people networking at events are just listening for the next moment when they can say something amazing. Which means they're not really listening.

Years ago, I was at a conference where I had to speak on stage after this gentleman who was extremely charismatic. In terms of theater and performance, I could not match him. He was like a rock star, complete with the tattoos, disheveled hair, biker boots, sunglasses and leather jacket. At one point, he even took off his leather jacket and threw it on the ground. It was really dramatic.

During his talk, though, I remember thinking, "He's almost speaking *through* the audience, as if they're not there at all. He's speaking *over* the audience, not *to* them." He was acting.

He had also come into the conference right before he had to give his speech. But I had been there for two days. I had been listening to all the speakers and all the audience questions. Plus, I had been talking to people, so by the time I took the stage after the rock star speaker finished his presentation, I wanted to reset the tone.

The company I work for is Japanese owned, so I started by bowing to the audience. Then I said, "I'm very glad to be here from a Japanese-owned company, and because of that, we're going to take a different tone now." I then started to repeat some things that I had heard throughout the conference. I related those statements to my talk in order to acknowledge that there were some common challenges people in the audience were facing. When possible, I would make eye contact with the people who had asked me those specific questions when we spoke earlier in the day. I wanted them to feel that I listened first in order to speak.

After I finished giving my speech, a few people came up to me and said that what I talked about was extremely useful to them. They knew how to go back to their organization and do something differently or start something new.

Their comments about the rock star were, "Wow, he was amazing." And of course, everyone wanted to get a beer with him because he was so magnetic. Heck, I wanted to party with him, too. They enjoyed his performance. But did they feel like he cared? Was he helpful?

For my speech, the response was different and, I believe, better—or at least more actionable. I listened. I remembered what people said. I met them where they were, and by doing so, I also met some of their needs.

In short, I wasn't acting. I was helpful.

Thinking back to my childhood for a moment, I listened to my grandfather and helped where he needed it, whether it was driving a truck or spending time with him, in silence, sitting in rocking chairs on the front porch with a cold glass of iced tea as he watched the world go by for a few moments' rest. At an early age, I realized that if I was going to thrive in that family and community, it was all about them and not about me. I was creative. I could draw, paint and build. I could find solutions to other people's problems. I could fit in and help.

There's another saying in the South, "If you don't have anything nice to say, come sit beside me." The Brits would call this being cheeky. Some of what I say in this book may sound like tough advice, but if it does nothing more than spark a debate, it will have been helpful. If you totally disagree with me, then at least you will have refined your position. These words are here to help.

How can a brand accustomed to being the repetitive and authoritative voice switch roles to that of being an attentive, listening helper—and thereby increase its relevance to consumers?

That's what you'll learn in this book. Let's discover how your company or your client's company can become a listening brand.

PART ONE

IDENTIFYING THE PROBLEM

WHY YOU THINK YOU'RE LISTENING BUT YOU'RE LIKELY NOT

CHAPTER 1

WHO IS HOLDING THE MEGAPHONE?

There's no easy way to say this.

In terms of time and budget, many companies today are wasting enormous resources on traditional brand-oriented marketing. They take a lot of time and money to make stuff and push it at consumers.

It's a sinking ship, and throwing money at it to make it better is, as they say, like rearranging the deck chairs on the Titanic.

Let's look at why that is, and how you can begin turning that ship around.

From Being Retail Focused to Relationship Focused

It's all about the unique cultures and lives of the consumers you want to reach, not the product category you compete within. I'll talk more about this in much more detail later on, but when I first started my career in advertising, brands listened to customers and prospects by holding focus groups, conducting market research, doing stakeholder interviews and preparing post-advertising campaign reports within an industry category (or perhaps in a related one). So many of our proposals back then included about 15 stakeholder interviews, 30 customer on-on-ones and a few focus groups in the most important markets. Rarely did we use statistically significant research, and we didn't have access to digital data like we do today. Some companies had brand trackers or depended on other agencies' popular brand-ranking studies, but none of these were truly robust when you peered under the hood, and none had access to digital and social data. While current brand trackers may be more robust in including proper digital data, they still focus on ranking scale and strength—a hindsight viewpoint. When it came to identifying how to help an individual brand, the tactics were almost always based on qualitative research.

There were—and still are—some fundamental problems with these market research methods.

For one thing, almost all depend on individuals' self-reporting of information, which can be way off course, as we'll see soon. These methods also assume, for the most part, that people make their purchasing decisions by comparing similar items or similar brands to one another. In that scenario, the item with the best benefits—whether tangible or intangible—wins. They also ignore people's unconscious, unspoken motivations.

What we're seeing now, though, is that people make their purchasing decisions from an entirely different perspective. For instance, if I'm thinking about purchasing a car, a soft drink or a running shoe, I'm generally not thinking about which one has the best brakes, the best fizz or the best cushioning. In reality, I'm usually thinking about the brand I've always thought about—the one I know the best, the one I see most often, or the one my friend has or likes.

In other words, I'm thinking about a product within the context of my cultural group. I'm thinking about the brand that I have a cultural connection to—a relationship.

By the time I've decided to buy a pair of running shoes, let's say, my decision rarely has anything to do with the tangible features of the shoe: questions that a company might ask in traditional market research.

Instead, my decision has to do with the brands that my friends consider, which may be only one or two. I'll choose the brand that's right for me, yes, but it's also dependent on who I am—how I'm positioned—within my cultural group. I'll think, consciously or unconsciously, about the brand that plays a role in my circle: in the lives of my friends and family.

You'll rarely have someone go into a shoe store and say, "I want the best pair of running shoes." A few people will do that, but more often than not, someone will walk into the Nike store or go onto the Nike website because that particular brand has been on their mind and discussed in their circle. It's already part of their world.

What does this idea of "cultural relationship" mean in terms of utilizing a company's marketing and market research resources?

Many companies are recognizing that they have been wasting money, but they may not know exactly how or why. And truthfully, some of the old methods can still produce useful answers—to a point. For example, asking consumers questions about the context and category your company is in, and about some of the tangible benefits of your product or service, is key because you've still got to get all the basics right.

But today, the importance of those results is hugely exaggerated.

The fact is, we can get much richer answers now by looking at social media, search engine behavior and Internet usage: the data that people generate as they move across the web or use their phones.

Even more, we can see answers to questions we wouldn't have even known to ask by looking at people's actual behaviors.

When a brand isn't investing in new tools and teams designed specifically for listening in this way, it can find itself mired in at least two forms of waste: money (and time) spent solely on old-school market research methods; and in turn, traditional brand-oriented advertising based on the results of that old-school research. It's no wonder that companies are seeing diminishing returns on their investment.

Case in point: the two largest global soft drink brands, soft drink Brand A vs. soft drink Brand B.

In this matchup, Brand A is improving, but Brand B is still winning—because they hopped onto the listening trend first.

Tradition vs. Today

Until recently, Brand A had been doing its market research mostly in the traditional way, as we just talked about. They get the results and hand them over to a big agency. Carrying on in that tradition, the big agency comes into the picture with an advertising campaign based on the results of the market research.

After the campaign is ready, Brand A goes to its local markets—countries and regions around the world—and only then does it ask those teams if they want to use the campaign.

Well naturally, some of those teams say no, they don't want to use the ad campaign. They feel the broad idea in the campaign doesn't reflect their unique market situation. While sometimes this is an attempt to protect their role and mandate, it is often correct. Rarely does that global team take a great deal of time to deeply understand the consumers in those markets, thus the output is a miss.

Instead of hearing even more "cha-ching," Brand A has wasted time, energy and money on something that isn't even going to be used.

To make matters worse, the local market Brand A teams that do agree to use the new advertising simply put it in front of people, full stop: well-scripted videos, billboards, print ads, digital banner ads, all on display for the world to see. They just follow orders as they were given.

You know this scenario all too well. These messages are pushed out, put out, promoted and played. Every one of them has the "right" colors, the "right" wording, the "right" imagery and the "right" music that is supposed to persuade people to buy Brand A. After all, that's what the market research told them to do...right?

Maybe not, as we'll see in this book.

What about the countries that choose not to use the globally created assets? What do they do?

They develop their own advertising for their local market, which leads to even more production budget being wasted. And they use this advertising in the exact same way: shoved in front of people with the hopes that the audience will think, "Oh my gosh, that ad is so beautiful and amazing. I love Brand A! I must have a cold can of Brand A right now!"

This scheme just doesn't work so well anymore. Brand A knows this now, but it's a little late in this face-to-face marketing showdown. Sorry, Brand A, but Brand B has been topping the pop charts for a long time here.

While still using some old-school market research and advertising methods, Brand B has been shifting a significant amount of its budget into local markets, countries and regions. Those teams take the money they would have spent in the way Brand A's teams did, and instead they spend it in an entirely different way—using social media.

YouTube, Facebook, Twitter, Instagram, Snapchat: these platforms are prime targets for effective advertising because they have created user-generated celebrities. So what do the local Brand B teams do? They ask these locally grown social media celebrities to do something unique with their brand.

The celebrity might talk about how Brand B has been a part of the world they live in—how it's been useful to them. In this case, "useful" might mean something as simple as alleviating boredom, giving them energy or providing a beverage to refresh them while they play video games.

The major difference here is the idea of brand-generated content versus user-generated content targeted to local markets. It's about capitalizing—literally and figuratively— on that area's cultural sensibilities.

And in terms of the role for the global Brand B team, they work with those big media companies to strike deals and get access to new innovations, their approved partners, and— even better—free creative work that can be scaled across all markets. The global team's role is no longer about making stuff; it's about getting access to stuff and making great deals.

Which method do you think has been more effective: Brand A's or Brand B's?

It seems obvious when it's spelled out this way.

But so many companies still don't see it.

They continue to develop marketing and advertising strategy based on the old methodology: do market research, create a campaign based on the results, run the campaign and then expect money to magically appear in the bank.

Does it still work? Sometimes.

More and more, though, it's failing to produce the results companies have come to expect.

In the case of Brand B, these targeted, local social media videos and other content have been highly successful. The number of views and shares they receive demonstrates that they are far outperforming the videos where a brand has tried to create the perfectly scripted, beautiful—but traditional—ad. And keep in mind, views and shares mean that people are seeing and thinking about your product; thus consciously or unconsciously, you are on their mind when they are faced with a beverage choice.

Brand A has been very slow to see this and hasn't moved

quickly. Especially with a younger audience, Brand B is clearly winning.

The Megaphone is Changing Hands

Let's take a brief turn back to the past. In 1928, Edward Bernays, the pioneer of public relations, said, "The conscious and intelligent manipulation of the organized habits and opinions of the masses is an important element in democratic society. Those who manipulate this unseen mechanism of society constitute an invisible government, which is the true ruling power of our country. We are governed, our minds are molded, our tastes are formed, our ideas suggested, largely by men we have never heard of. This is a logical result of the way in which our democratic society is organized."

Bernays laid the groundwork for what has been the prominent way for brands to influence the masses: control the megaphone, and you can control the people. By "control," I mean get them to think and act as you want for the benefit of your brand.

Times are changing. People have caught on to this invisible power, and they don't like it. There has been a big shift.

The megaphone is changing hands.

Today, the voice of the people is doing a better job of delivering for a brand in the social/digital world than the brand itself.

Let me repeat that: The people can now deliver the brand's message more effectively than the brand itself.

This is no small thing. It's truly a paradigm shift in advertising and marketing.

Remember, the old way started with market research, weeks of ideation, and then focus groups to see what version of your campaign seemed most popular. Then you'd go into high production periods, shooting, re-editing and making your ad seem perfect.

And let's not forget media placement: another major cost. As we just saw, what you produce may not even be used by the local markets, so the whole process has to start again there.

In a traditional branding agency, you're trying to develop the voice of corporation or its brand. You're not telling them anything at all about listening, relating to or being sensitive to consumers. You're not teaching them how to build rapport. Instead, you're telling the corporation how to say the same thing into the megaphone every day until people believe it.

It's costly, exhausting and ultimately, it's not very effective anymore.

Jumping back to Brand B for a moment, let's sum up its new process in the simplest way possible.

1. It figures out who its customers listen to.

2. It asks if those people, or even other brands, will speak on Brand B's behalf (for a fee, of course).

That's it.

Approach advertising this way, and you save time and money, and you generate much better results. You're looking toward the voices of your customer's peers—as opposed to the voice of a corporation—to connect with them.

This is a game-changing moment for brands that advertise.

Check that.

This is *the* game-changing moment for brands that advertise.

Does traditional advertising still have a role to play? For the moment, yes. There's still a need to reach those people who can be hard to reach. Not all consumers are following Instagram celebrities. Not all consumers check Facebook many times a day. Not all consumers subscribe to YouTube videos—even though with young people, it certainly seems like all of them are.

And let's not forget that social networks like Facebook are now charging for a share of the audience. They know the value of something being shared, so companies need to put money behind content that used to be free so that it shows up in someone's social feed. Organic sharing is still happening, too, so it's really a mixture of companies paying their way to get into someone's feed, and people who share having an influence within their cultural group.

Otherwise, though, traditional advertising is generally a waste of money. Today, most people spend many hours on their phone using apps, and those spaces have very few advertising options. In fact, 80 percent of the time

Americans spend on their increasingly smart phones is within only five apps. Repeat, only five apps. And those apps are Facebook, YouTube, Google Maps, Gmail and Pandora. It's important to note that browser activity is not within an app. If we consider that, we see that people spend a great deal of time within the Google universe.

Simply put, there just aren't many effective advertising formats left to communicate in the one-way, overtly branded style of the past.

Let's look for a moment at what these spaces—such as mobile phones—do have, though: places to consume content. Pictures. Videos. Articles. When a brand listens to its customers in these spaces by viewing data, it can understand its customers much better. It can build relationships and provide content around topics its customers love.

Traditional ads may never totally disappear, but there will be a shift from ads being around the periphery of the content, to the ads being the content itself. This will especially increase as consumers, and even the big media players, start to embrace ad blockers—software that prevents digital ads popping up when you browse. We even see the Apple and iOS universe warming to the idea that traditional digital ads are blocked in browsing spaces; thus, content and collaboration with the apps and companies named above will become more and more important (with the exception of Pandora, which is very US centric). So if people spend a great deal of their free time in smartphone spaces and ad blockers are increasing, and there are few big media players to work with who just so happen to be highly social platforms, how does traditional advertising fit in? Well, it doesn't, really.

The successful brands know that consumers are not just passive listeners anymore. They're definitely not passive consumers. In terms of advertising today, brands now serve at the pleasure of the consumer in highly social spaces.

The consumer is standing on top of the mountain with the megaphone in their hand, and the brand is in the valley below, listening to the message.

Is it too late for your brand to get into the game? Not at all. In fact, making this shift also makes it hypothetically possible for a company to have zero waste and balance out earlier losses. In the next chapter, we'll look at a simple shift you can make to become a brand that listens, starting now.

What You Heard in This Chapter

- Companies are likely wasting enormous resources, in terms of their time and budget, on traditional brand-oriented marketing—and seeing diminishing returns.

- Leveraging user-generated content will bring a greater return on investment today that brand-created content because the megaphone has changed hands: the voice of the people is speaking on behalf of the brand.

- When a brand listens to their consumers in online spaces by using data, they better understand what they like; then they can build relationships with consumers and also provide content around the topics their consumers love.

Try This

What is an example of a brand that you particularly like that you believe is doing a great job of listening to consumers and relating to their needs and/or culture? What evidence shows you that they're paying attention?

CHAPTER 2

WHAT TO DO FIRST? BE CURIOUS

Right this very minute, your customers are talking to you.

Can you hear them? Do you know how they feel about you?

Whether it's obvious to you or not, customers are telling you what they want, directly or indirectly. Today, the listening channel is mostly an indirect one, giving you information that customers didn't necessarily have an easy way to share with you before. Let's explore this idea in this chapter.

With social media and the data that comes from people's movement, activities and behavior online, you can hear the voice of the people. You can actually hear their wants, needs and interests by what they do online, without them speaking a word directly to you.

You just have to be trained in how and where to look and

listen—and understand which questions provide the best answers.

Even if it seems like you're entering this game a bit late, don't worry. The idea that it's too late to get into anything in the world of strategic communications? Well, it's just not something to be concerned with. Everything is moving so fast. In a year, we'll be playing a different game. We're all chasing an ever-shifting goal post.

Yes, there's some learning that has to take place. But the tools and systems we have available to us today—that the savvy brands are using to listen to customers and prospects—are going to continue to evolve and change. They'll have to, because technology is changing minute to minute. All you have to do is look at how quickly new social platforms take hold. Like Snapchat, for instance, which didn't exist three years ago and now is the latest and greatest, at least in the Western world. It may be gone next year, or it may be the next Facebook or WeChat. No one knows.

Lessen the Guesswork

I'm approaching this topic from the angle of working at a big digital media agency, and what we try to do for our clients is to take the guesswork out of everything: I mean everything from who should you target, what are they saying, what should you do, where should you be. And all supported by serious, factual data—not intuition. We're endeavoring to get a good return on investment for our clients: to stop the waste and show them where to put their money so that it will go much, much further.

This is what I want to do for you with this book.

What can you do, starting today? Something simple.

All a brand really needs to do, to start getting a greater return, is adopt an attitude of extreme curiosity. With deep curiosity, you can be right on the forefront of the next big thing even if you've never tried any of this before.

So it's just two words for you to remember: Be curious.

As we talked about in chapter 1, many companies are not challenging themselves to change their business strategies in kind or in degree with the massive shifts taking place in marketing and communications.

They're often only asking questions related to what they should be saying to their customers—questions about imagery and messaging they believe will appeal to them.

They're also asking questions about how they're different from the competitors in their category. For example, they're wondering about things like, "Do customers prefer green or yellow?" "Do they prefer great suspension, or do they prefer aggressive design?"

It may not seem like it, but really, this information is irrelevant to their current or potential customers today. There are inherent problems with starting with questions like these.

Companies are already assuming—important word, "assuming"—that people compare things within the same category: for instance, that they compare your car to other cars when they're deciding to purchase. They're assuming that people are visiting one car company's website to see how great the suspension is on car X, and then going to another car company's website to see how great the suspension is on car Y.

As I've been alluding to, this is not how most customers make decisions today. And even though they're based on questioning, these kinds of assumptions are built into the questions and are not fueling the extreme curiosity required to build a brand in this new environment.

Pulling back for a broader view, we can see that companies locked in the traditional mode of investigation are thinking within their category only, instead of thinking within their consumers' culture. In doing so, they're relying on information they're comfortable with—staying inside their own house rather than venturing outside.

It's almost like they're agoraphobic when it comes to data that reveals consumer culture. They're relying on their own surveys, their own studies, their own segmentation, their own experts, their own context. They're not pushing themselves to get out of their own heads and get into the lives and heads of the people that they want to reach.

So what should they be doing? What questions demonstrate the type of extreme curiosity I'm talking about?

We will go into this in much more detail throughout this

book. But they should be asking questions about lifestyle relevancy, i.e., culture: how their brand fits in vis-à-vis other habits, hobbies and interests of the customer.

And most companies are not asking an even more important, basic question: Do the customers we want, in return, want to hear anything from us—at all?

Question Every Assumption

Step even further back, and we can see that in fact, companies need to question absolutely everything they're doing right now. Everything. They need to be willing to look outside of their own comfort zone for answers they don't even know they need.

Will your current customers make you money in the future?

Do you even know who is likely to buy your product?

Are your targets realistic at all?

Let's consider a hypothetical scenario.

You are working with an automotive client in your market. Your client comes to you and says, "We have this car model, and we want to sell it to millennials: young, cool, hip people, preferably males."

Let's look at the ramifications of a statement like that from this new vantage point. What are the assumptions the client already made? Lots. We'll begin with some key questions to elicit the most helpful answers.

First, are you even starting this conversation with the right audience? Meaning, do you know that the people you've selected are actually the people who will want to buy what you're trying to sell?

Note that "millennials" is a vague word for a vast audience, but I digress.

This automotive company may—or may not, we'll find out in a moment—have determined correctly who would be interested in buying this particular car model. There's a difference between designing something that you *hope* will appeal to a large group, versus designing something that you *know* will appeal to a large group. Don't assume that the product design team really understands who will warm to the product. From toothpaste to automobiles, always make sure the interested audience is actually there and of a size that will help you meet your sales targets.

After you've determined whether you're targeting the right audience, you need to ask this question: Are you using the best methods to reach them?

For example, if you're trying to sell a car to cool, hip male millennials and you're spending money developing and placing TV commercials, you may be missing your target audience altogether because they're not even watching TV. In fact, they may not even own a TV.

There's a third question to ask once you've answered the first two sufficiently: How can we encourage a positive response that can build momentum—something that takes on a life its own online? Answering this one requires some of the extreme curiosity I mentioned earlier, along with creativity.

OK, so back to the automotive client. When you get curious and start listening and looking at who is online talking about—or searching for—this car, you may find something unexpected.

Perhaps it's women, not men, who are expressing interest in the car.

And it isn't women millennials, either, but middle-aged women with children who are scrutinizing a particular safety feature in the car.

If this is the case, you have really missed the mark.

Here's the lesson: Before we can even begin to figure out the most effective ways to reach an audience, we need to use data to see if we're even talking to the right people in the first place. Once we understand exactly who this audience is, we do some research by looking at data that comes from their online movements and activities to see what they're doing, where they're going, and how they're interacting with websites, media, content or videos—and even how they're interacting with one another. After we know where they spend their time, we start to listen to what they are saying in those spaces.

Why do we do all of this extensive data-based research?

To deeply understand what is most relevant and useful for them inside the world that these people inhabit.

To see what their actions tell us about their interests, their likes and dislikes, and about the way they consume information and products.

Only then do we even begin to think about what we might want to say to them—if anything at all.

This is very different from declaring, "We have a new car that we want to sell to hip, male millennials that has cool colors and awesome headlights" and putting that into an expensive TV ad, crossing your fingers and hoping for the best. This is making sure the interested audience is there and that you're speaking with them in a way that will surely resonate.

It Seems Obvious, But...

As obvious and simple as it looks when I spell it out this way, this curiosity-based listening process is what most companies still do not do. The automotive case I explained was a hypothetical. But I have worked with clients that literally didn't know that the people they were targeting weren't the same people willing to embrace and buy their product. Everything they did in communications was focusing on a consumer that couldn't care less. In recent years, this consumer seems to have been a "millennial" a lot of the time.

In short, companies that are sliding off the deck of the Titanic are asking questions about their competitors and about their own products, instead of asking themselves how they can be more relevant to their customers—once they know who those customers are.

Here's the amazing thing about all of this: If it weren't for social media, there wouldn't be a way to know that an entirely different culture, an entirely different group of people on a massive scale, is talking about this car. You just can't determine that without the data you get from social media.

The old ways of segmenting—interviewing people and asking experts—can only get you so far. Human beings are wildly unpredictable, and those old kinds of questioning methods cannot tell you what human behavior online can reveal.

There's a great story of a woman who had been a loyal customer of a mobile carrier for several years. One day, she posted a message on social media about a competitive brand's offer. She wrote something along the lines of, "I wish my current carrier OmniTel would match the plan from All-Mobile." It was a simple post—that only used the handle of her current carrier—OmniTel.

Well, AllMobile, the one that had the plan she liked, saw her post and did a little research. They discovered that this woman was a huge fan of Jon Bon Jovi. So they responded to her with this message: "Sounds like you're living on a prayer... If you get off the lost highway I'd be happy to have a chat. Have a nice day—AllMobile. " If you are not a Bon Jovi fan, those are bits of copy from his songs.

How were they able to do this?

Clearly, AllMobile had amazing staff and/or tools to listen to people on social media—even when the message was not directly to them. Then, they took time to get to know a bit about her, and they responded quickly in a way that related to her interests and culture: referring to popular songs by Bon Jovi.

It wasn't until much later that current carrier, OmniTel, replied to her and without any sense of humor or understanding. They simply replied in a corporate way—and it was too little, too late. They weren't moving fast enough to listen and respond appropriately. They were not acting like they cared.

What happened? I'll bet you can guess.

The woman switched her allegiance: no small feat in the mobile phone carrier business. These customers sign contracts for long-term relationships, and people stick with the same company for many, many years. The fact that doing just a little bit of listening and using a human touch with a sense humor could get this woman to change her cell phone carrier contract is pretty powerful. And that change won't just lead to a bit more money this year: she will probably become a long-term customer. Heck, she will probably tell other people about her positive experience with AllMobile and their clever response. What's important to take away is that while this was a largely manual intervention—someone messaged her on social media—this will become more and more automated over time. One day, the interventions will be done by algorithms, but if a company is not prepared to think this way, they will miss the big opportunity.

Another example of a listening brand involves the two biggies in the burger world: McDonald's and Burger King. Cue the "McWhopper."

Someone at Burger King had the idea to bring these two companies together to make a sandwich for Peace One Day, a nonprofit organization that wishes to have September 21 as annual Peace Day around the world.

In other words, One Day, One Burger: a united front for peace as demonstrated by these two huge companies that normally compete with one another.

After hearing about Burger King's idea, McDonald's CEO acknowledged the effort and took it seriously. In the end, though, McDonald's CEO said "no" to the idea, but he also said that they appreciated it very much. I can understand why McDonald's didn't go for it because of course, Burger King would benefit from the publicity more than McDonald's would. But what I thought was nice about it was that the CEOs got involved in the conversation. They were paying attention, and they were listening.

That's a sign of how brands are having to act differently today. When something starts to get some chatter and buzz, companies have to jump in. They can't stay removed anymore.

Human Behavior Isn't Always Rational

The singer Bjork has a song called "Human Behavior" with a line that says, "If you ever get close to a human and human behavior, be ready, be ready to get confused."

We marketers like to think that we have great intuition, but the fact is, our gut is sometimes wrong, and being wrong can cost a lot of time and money. We can't always have our finger on the pulse. But when you're able to look at digital and social data that's generated by millions of people's daily activity online, you can really have amazing insights. Epiphanies, even.

But they're often inexplicable by anything resembling logic. They simply are what they are, facts in and of themselves. The data reveal the unexpected in human behavior.

Can companies continue to do what they've always done? Sure, but they shouldn't expect good growth or return. This digital and social world, and all the data that comes with it, is the new reality we're living in.

On the farm when I was growing up, we might have wanted to grow corn every year at a maximum yield because it was easy for us to do. But if that wasn't what people were buying, our farm would have become irrelevant and eventually, we wouldn't have been putting food on our own tables.

Just like on the farm, if companies want to stay relevant and compete in the marketplace, they will have to adapt. If they don't want to change, then there are plenty of their peers that will, and they'll do it fast.

As I'm writing this book, there have been strikes by taxi drivers from the UK to France because they're unhappy about the rise and threat of Uber. Some of those concerns are valid, especially when it comes to taxation, insurance and proper training. But for the traditional taxi drivers, it's not enough to simply stick your heels into the ground and refuse to change or adapt.

This is the voice of the people speaking. If the people didn't want the service that Uber is offering, Uber would not be in business and succeeding.

Looking toward the future, I would bet that ultimately, these taxi driver strikes won't be successful. Why? Because the taxi companies are trying to tell the people—potential customers—that their needs are wrong. It's not going to work.

The success of Uber is the voice of the masses telling the status quo that their needs aren't being met. I've had the same experience, myself. I would get into a taxi in London and want to use my bank card, and the driver would say, "No credit cards. Cash only today." If you don't have cash, you get out of the taxi and call an Uber.

But unlike when you're driving a car or taxi, you can't simply put your company into reverse. You have to adapt and evolve. For those businesses that refuse to do so, they're going to be working with a limited, niche audience, on a smaller scale that shares the value of not being extremely connected to social media and a digital economy. That's the reality, and it's probably not where most companies want to be.

In the next chapter, we'll delve even more deeply into why this shift from traditional market research and ad creation, to a new strategy borne from getting curious and observing human behavior, is essential to building a competitive brand today.

What You Heard in This Chapter

- The best way to enter the game of listening to data is simply to develop extreme curiosity.

- Brands that are falling behind are not challenging themselves to change their businesses in kind or in degree with the massive shifts in marketing and communications today.

- Category context of a product or service doesn't matter nearly as much as the cultural context of the consumer.

Try This

In addition to Uber, what's an example of a brand that is responding to consumer demand in a very disruptive way? What cultural context are they paying attention to?

CHAPTER 3

WHAT KIND OF LISTENING ARE YOU DOING?

You may be saying, "But we *are* listening, JR. We're spotting trends, testing ideas, getting feedback. What else are we supposed to do?"

But here's the thing: Why are you doing all those tasks? To develop the perfect, beautiful commercial? To craft the most persuasive tagline? To figure out which features matter most?

If that's your end goal, you've got the wrong "why." That's a big part of what we'll talk about in this chapter.

Because this game is no longer about what you want to say. It's about what the consumer wants to hear and where they want to hear it.

Let me put that another way.

Companies are doing—and paying mightily for—all that market research just so they can design the perfect "big idea": the magically persuasive line of copy, imagery or animation that will win people over. It's all about creating an opportunity to say something, and say it loudly.

This is old school—and nearly irrelevant—research. And here's an example of why it can backfire, big time, in the service of creating that almighty message.

Until fairly recently, self-reporting has been the standard way of getting insights from people you'd like to reach: people filling out a survey, for example, or a company conducting a focus group. No matter how you safeguard it, these types of tools will have human error. Simply put, they aren't reliable.

Several years ago, for two days the agency I worked for (in the pre-digital days) held focus groups in Russia related to a client's product. After a while, we realized that we were getting answers that seemed totally out of context related to the socio-economic status of the people we were interviewing. We knew that they were working-class people, but their answers sounded really amazing for that demographic. For example, they would say, "When I grow up, I'm going to have a luxury car, a wife and kids, and two houses. And I'm going to take holidays to the French Riviera in the summer." Or we'd ask about what they do for fun, and they'd answer, "I go horseback riding on the weekend, or I take my family to the lake, or I go to restaurants and exclusive clubs, or I take my bike or luxury car out for a spin."

What were we missing? A major cultural nuance, that's what.

To talk with complete honesty about your life in Russia is not a social norm. Back then, at least, to tell the truth about things like that would have been out of character. Instead, the cultural norm was to project the type of person you wanted people to think you are—not the type of person you actually are.

Biases and Nuances

This Russian focus group example is key because it points to a huge error that often goes unnoticed. In self-reporting market research, people often give answers that they believe will impress other people or answers that cause them less dissonance. This is especially true in focus groups, where people also tend to follow a sort of "group mentality." If one person starts to talk about their amazing vacations, for instance, someone else will talk about their own amazing vacation—even if it's not true. There's a competitiveness that develops within the group.

What else can this Russia story illustrate? It shows that this type of research, and the understanding that we think we're gleaning from it, can be deeply flawed. The problem is, we don't necessarily know when it's flawed and when it isn't. We knew that it was wrong in Russia because after the focus groups, one of my colleagues explained to me that in that particular cultural context, it was normal for people to exaggerate. At that point, my internal monologue seriously questioned why were doing the groups in the first place.

People are far too nuanced to be lumped together into big categories, which is what limits most traditional market research. Our ability to watch human behavior through data analysis—confusing as that behavior may be, at times—demonstrates this complexity, one kilobyte at a time. The notion that one "big" message will resonate with everyone who is looking at your car or your soft drink is backwards thinking. Each individual has their own reason, within their own culture, for potentially wanting a product. Looking for the "big idea" will average out what doesn't need to be averaged anymore.

Listening for a New Purpose

Don't keep looking in reverse or trying to predict the future. Look at the present moment. Look at what people are telling you right now, this very minute, through their behavior.

Then, instead of doing all this research to develop the "perfect" message that relates to everyone so that you can say something to them, you need to listen to people first to understand both their differences and their similarities. You may find, for example, that you need to quietly say a hundred different things to a hundred different groups of people. Don't freak out, because it's doable with the right technology and skilled people.

Looking in this direction changes the way you will think about developing a "campaign," which ultimately may be completely inappropriate and ineffective. Why spend many months—and many dollars—developing this "big idea," meaning a big blast of messaging, when you could spread your budget out across a year listening to the people you've discovered are important? Then you'll be able to test different communications with different groups, always with a focus on being helpful to them, with the ultimate aim of getting a groundswell of social support.

Think of the image of the consumer now being on the mountaintop. They are holding the megaphone now, with the company brand below them, listening to what the consumer is saying. The consumer climbed the mountain through a groundswell of support from their cultural group. That's what swept them up there. If you want to rise to the top along with them, you need people advocating for you and inviting you into that stream of support.

This can be a tough thing to hear, but brands are no longer leading the charge. The people are.

Here's a wild analogy for you, but I think it illustrates this point quite well. When we look at why the communist revolution happened in China, we can see that it was partly because Mao Zedong went village by village with his message, speaking with individual after individual and engaging with small communities. He connected on a human level with people in those small communities, and eventually those groups led him to the city centers, and so on.

He didn't try to win over a massive city first. He made himself relevant to individuals, and the movement and message grew from there on its own.

You don't start by screaming your message from the top of the tower. You actually go to people and listen to them. You get to know them by walking alongside them—just as I did when I worked alongside my grandfather all those years ago. Once you've shown your value in the form of being helpful, those people need to be encouraged to advocate on your behalf.

Shouting Louder Doesn't Work Anymore

Believe me, I know this might seem scary. But whether it's scary or not, whether we like it or not, companies have no other choice but to try to win people's trust and loyalty in this new way. If they continue to shout at consumers, they will alienate them and fall further behind their competitors who are using data to pay attention.

As we've talked about, there are times when overtly obvious advertising is needed. There's something to be said for creating an inspirational image, for example. Sometimes you need to see a beautiful car ad because it demonstrates that the brand is legitimate enough and professional enough to afford a billboard in Times Square. These ads can be a sign of stature and expertise.

But—and this is a big "but"—they can't be the only way a company communicates. These types of ads have a role to play, but it's a much less important one today than it has ever been.

Even in the glory days of Mad Men, peer-to-peer trust has

always been the most important element of building a brand. It's really the Holy Grail of commerce. If you're trying to reach someone, the best way to persuade them is to get the person they trust the most to tell them what you want them to believe. We trust our family and we trust our close friends more than we would ever trust a corporation. But only in the last five years or so has social media really scaled to where most of us have 200 friends on our social network of choice. And those friends add up. Recently, Facebook celebrated having one billion people on their platform in a single day. That's one billion people with around 200 friends each. That's a lot of connections.

If we were to add up our social network connections— because we have one for friends and family, one for celebrities and personalities we follow, one for our careers, you name it—many of us have hundreds, or even thousands, of people influencing our views on life. And not just a little, but on an increasingly daily (or hourly) basis. It is projected that in 2016, three billion smart phone devices will be in usage—each of them with social platforms.

Fifteen or twenty years ago, we got our information from television news, the newspaper, print magazines and the advertising in those media. That's not how we're consuming information today. If we wanted someone's advice about something years ago, we asked them in person, on the telephone or by letter. Maybe the occasional fax (remember those?).

Social media has allowed our access to peer-to-peer trust to grow exponentially. Influencing that peer-to-peer trust—or someone would say manipulating that trust—is the business we're in now in advertising. We're still trying to persuade people to buy things, but this is the way to do it today.

Chew on This...

FreshDent makes chewy breath mints that are a lot like candy, and they wanted to persuade young people—ages 18 to 21—to use them. For months, they did market research and worked on perfecting a TV commercial that would convince young people to buy their breath mints.

At this point, our agency got involved and figured out pretty quickly that FreshDent had not been listening to consumer behavior. Case in point: young people today don't want anything to do with mints. It's not part of their culture. Then trying to reach them via a TV commercial is pointless because they probably don't even watch regular TV.

By paying attention to their behavior, we learned that they're not buying mints and candies in order to buy gum, instead. They're spending their money on games and songs to play on their phones. In other words, they're spending their small-purchase money on items that relate to their culture—not on something that makes their mouth feel sweeter or fresher. We also saw that they're not watching TV but hanging out on social media, largely Snapchat, Instagram, WeChat, Line.

FreshDent had only been paying attention to cues within their own category instead of cues coming from a lifestyle and culture—the relationship cues. In other words, talking about how your mint is the coolest, freshest and sweetest is totally irrelevant when your competition is a mobile game or the newest track from Miley Cyrus!

The whole point of being able to look at the way people move around online—the way they search for things or what they say and do on social media—is that it's their actual activity. It's transparent. It's a fact. No flaws, no errors. It's simple, incontrovertible proof. This kind of information is so much richer and so much more helpful because you're removing the erratic nature of human testimony and human intuition. You're studying their behavior, almost like an anthropologist would.

In fact, when I was at university I took a class called Practical Anthropology. My final project was to watch a preschool classroom for an entire semester in order to report back on their developmental behavior. I had to sit and observe the students through a two-way mirror and record everything that they did.

I had no hypothesis. I had no objective other than to report what I was seeing.

This is what data can do for us. It gives us the facts without any layering of assumptions on top of it.

FreshDent, the mint company, did figure out that their old agency was doing things wrong. After about a year of no results, the advertising agency and FreshDent parted ways, and we were brought in to play a bigger role.

(Quick aside: If you're working in the advertising industry and you're not paying attention to data-driven research, your job is definitely at risk.)

But FreshDent now has an extremely intelligent, clever and creative social listening and social media strategy for trying to make breath mints culturally relevant again. That's its objective now, as opposed to trying to prove that its mint is the best one over the other brands.

At this stage of our conversation about what it means to be a brand that listens, we should pause on an important point.

I worked in a traditional branding agency for six years, and they were six years when the most profound change in the industry occurred. I left that agency because I had an epiphany about the way brands had always been built in the past and how that wasn't going to work anymore. It was a big leap for me, but I went to an agency that focused on efficiency and data—which is not a natural "fit" for me, as you might guess from my background in psychology, human development and design.

I knew that if I was going to have a chance of staying relevant in this industry, I had to go in this new direction. I left an agency that was based on qualitative research and intuition, and went to an agency that is almost completely based on quantitative research and data-driven facts. It's like night and day.

I admit that it's still an uphill battle, even for me. After three years at a digital agency, I still come into work some days and say, "I don't understand the things that I should under-stand—I can't keep up!"

But you know what? I continue to learn. And apparently, my curiosity is working not just for me, but also for my clients. And it can work for you, too, when you start listening to data.

Before you can really understand this new way of doing things, I'd like to offer you a behind-the-scenes view of the way agencies used to work—and, frankly, the way some of them still do (maybe even yours). It's a methodology that doesn't serve anyone well today, and I'm a little sheepish about sharing it with you. But here goes in the next chapter...

What You Heard in This Chapter

- Companies may think they are listening by spotting trends, testing ideas and seeking feedback, but they're still performing these tasks in support of the expression of a "big idea."

- The old research methodology, which was developed to prepare to bombard the consumer (or even just to subtly nudge them), is being replaced by a new way of persuad-ing people based on trust.

- Social networks have expanded to such an extent that people have hundreds of friends, which constitute, in large part, the culture people listen to—consciously or subconsciously—when deciding what to buy.

Try This

What is an example of a company that you believe is really out of touch with consumers and may soon fail? Why?

CHAPTER 4

BACK TO BRAND BUILDING, CIRCA 2007

We've known each other for a few chapters now, and I have something important to tell you. I've alluded to it before, but looking at this today, it all seems so incredibly backwards to me. I can justify it by saying it was all we knew how to do, sure. But wow, does it ever look odd from where I sit now.

In this chapter, we're going to look closely at where I used to be in terms of brand building, the role of an agency in that process, and where we are—or where we should be—today.

If you're feeling like your company is wasting money, or if you're working with an agency that's struggling to produce a return on investment, this chapter might explain a whole lot to you. Or at least get you asking some new questions.

Remember the movie "Back to the Future"? It's time to get into your sleek, silver DeLorean automobile and set the date to 2007.

The "Old" Days (Not So Long Ago)

From 2007 to 2012, I was working for a top branding agency with offices all around the world. We were the best of the best, with a track record of branding the world's largest companies. The recession was approaching fast, and then it hit the United States and Europe hard, as we know. Dubai, as well, had a major real estate crisis. It was a pivotal time for everyone around the world, one that is still reverberating today as interest rates are at all-time lows and can't seem to get back up.

Over those years, the agency started to struggle. Fewer and fewer client briefs were landing on our desk, and for a long time, I couldn't figure out why. Part of it had to do with the economy, of course, but there seemed to be more behind it than that. Client requests were becoming miniscule: asking for logos, labels and names for new products, and that was about it. No brand analysis or strategy documents, nothing even approaching that level of agency involvement.

In those days, especially in pre-recession 2007-2008, we had a very detailed, specific way of working with clients. We would basically tell them, "If you'll allow us to find out what your brand is really about—what makes it compelling, true and differentiating—then we can help make your business successful."

We didn't have many proof points. The only way we could prove it was to talk about the "great brands" in a rather anecdotal way. But this never seemed to bother our clients, oddly enough. They trusted us. I think everyone admitted that there really wasn't a better way to build a brand at that time.

Our process with clients—no matter who they were or what industry they were in—always went something like this...

The overarching goal was to come up with a concise description of what made that particular company compelling. What differentiated it within its industry category? What would make people want it? And then we wrapped a bit of personality around that using imagery and tone.

We'd start the brand strategy process with "desk research," as we called it: looking around on the Internet—analyst reports, industry trends and not much else. Then we would look at the competition and try to understand what they were doing that seemed to work. Last, we'd do some stakeholder interviews, which pretty much meant talking to a few people at the client's company to see what they thought the brand should be about. Sometimes we would also interview consumers or hold focus groups. These would be made up of about 30 consumer interviews and three focus groups, which seemed to be the answer from small clients to big ones. Look online, chat with leaders, chat with consumers, hold some groups: that was our rigorous process.

Finally, we'd prepare a "brand model," which is one page with words describing what the brand stood for: a statement about its purpose. Often these things ended up looking like circles with different layers of copy—surely you have seen one before. If not, do a quick 'brand model' search. This brand model was supposed to magically guide the company toward becoming this amazing, compelling brand that people love and want. It was intended to guide internal communications as well as external communications. If companies would just get the right model, all would work out in the end and the company would thrive.

That's a lot for a one-pager to accomplish!

Speaking from a place now of complete humility, it's hard to quantify how much emphasis was placed on the brand model. We provided it to the client's advertising agency, public relations agency and people within the company: anyone who might need to be able to talk about the company.

You can probably guess what happened along the way. Remember the game of telephone you played in school? One person would whisper something into their friend's ear, and by the time the message snaked its way around the classroom, it would end up as something completely different from what it was when it started.

That's often what happened with the brand model. The message would get diluted, changed, possibly mangled. It would be interpreted and reinterpreted—for a fee, of course. Months, even years, were wasted trying to find a few words that would set the company on the right course to success.

The Scariest Part...

And what were we using to develop this brand model? This is the truly scary part.

Intuition. And I mean, a *lot* of intuition. To this day, I'm not even sure I could tell you what that means. We basically had a lot of smart and creative people that could figure out what the brand needed—but only to some degree, of course.

Clients were paying a lot of money for our intuition. They were put on hefty retainers and paid a fortune for not much more than a piece of paper, some imagery, templates and a logo. Always a logo.

Does this process sound familiar to you if you're a company or part of an agency?

Not only that, but this brand model continued to cost the client money by creating revenue streams for all these other agencies and employees involved in the branding process. When we handed the brand model over to the advertising agency, for example, the ad agency would often say, "This doesn't quite work for us, so we're going to have to reinterpret the message." And then they'd create this big, cumbersome process to "reinterpret" the brand—getting paid for their intuition.

The game of "telephone" continued. Same with the pr, digital, experiential, media agencies. Everyone charging for more 'creative strategy' and branding.

All of this busy-ness equaled more profits and revenue streams for these agencies and the conglomerates that owned them, but not much in the way of tangible results for the client.

On the agency side, the profit margin was high. Even so, it wasn't enough once the financial crisis hit. I believe we were hurt not because companies couldn't afford to pay us anymore, but because we didn't have anything more than our intuition to offer clients. We had nothing of measurable value, and that reality was revealed in stark terms.

In short, we couldn't advise them as to how to come out of the recession with anything more than what our "gut" told us.

We couldn't advise them on how to adapt to the increasing digitalization of the world.

We had no point of view on social media.

And it wasn't just us; it was all the branding agencies. The agency I worked for, which had been so in demand, became a place that just designed logos and provided design guidelines.

At least it felt that way.

Please don't get me wrong. This type of brand work has a purpose, but its impact has greatly diminished with the rise of the digital age.

Digital Begins Its Influence

When I look back, I can see that during those years I spent
at that traditional branding agency—again, that was from
2007 to 2012—digital advertising started to become more
sophisticated and social media scaled. It became more
important and integrated into what companies and agencies
were doing. What's so great is that when you run or serve a
digital ad or when you do anything at all in the digital space
in terms of advertising, you're also discovering something
at the same time.

It's not as if you simply put an ad on a website and it just sits
there, staring at the consumer. When they do click on that ad,
you know about it, and you know when they didn't click on
it. You're getting a straightforward data response telling you
a lot of information, like the number of people responding
to the ad, the type of people who are looking at it, the type
of people not responding to the ad, what else they've been
looking at, and what other things they like.

Suddenly, the brand-building process has become a whole
new landscape, one loaded with fact-based insights instead
of intuition. As a result, the entire branding process can be
flipped around. No intuition needed, either.

If you're working with an intelligent, digital- and social
media-savvy agency, then they have the ability to see very
deeply into consumer behavior. They can observe consumers you think you want and consumers who already want
you. They can tell you what their interests and needs are,
and where and how they move online. They can tell you

what they say, the tone, the imagery they like, the celebrities they follow.

If you can imagine it, you can see it.

Looking at this data and really being able to interpret it can tell you what your brand should be saying and how your brand should be acting. You don't need intuition anymore. The agencies that have depended so much on their creative intuition—their charisma, basically—are becoming less relevant.

Even Sir Martin Sorrell, the CEO of WPP plc. and sort of a hero in our industry, has made this point. It was around the time I left the traditional branding agency that he started saying that the industry was shifting from "Mad Men" to "Math Men." Why? Because the science and the associated rigor is now more important, more robust and more advanced than the artistic, creative side of the agency equation. And if you look at WPP's annual report, you can see that those agencies that are digital and data based are making up a huge portion of their revenue. In contrast, the companies that are heavily based on intuition-based creativity are eating into overall profits.

Building a Brand Today

How should a company build a brand today?

Reverse the process.

Do the opposite of what you used to do—seriously.

If I were to break it down into the simplest possible steps, it might look like this:

1. Use your current digital and social campaigns to figure out what your brand is about. Learn as much as you can by listening to digital data, with the help of experts in this field—maybe it's your digital, social or media agency. Remember, every digital interaction tells you more.

2. With that knowledge, find opportunities to build rapport and be helpful to consumers: both to those you knew cared about you, and those you didn't know cared about you. Get to know this audience closely. Follow them.

3. Create communications and partnerships that speak to those people and intervene when the moment is right.

If need be, hire consultants who can help you develop a story and imagery that will resonate with consumers based on what you've learned about who they are and what they really want.

That last group might be people who used to be strong in traditional branding, and honestly, they should be coming into the picture at the very end of this process. First and foremost, start with people who have the ability to read and understand digital and social data: people who can help you listen to your consumers. Those people who really "get" data are the most important in the brand-building process today.

Are You Sitting Down?

I actually have a quick and rather quirky example to share. It's one of the earliest I can remember of a company doing something in response to repeated requests from consumers: requests that were only tangentially related to its product (and that's a stretch!).

Remember, brands should be about helping, not saying things.

Procter and Gamble's Charmin toilet paper brand released an online tool—which is now an app, by the way—called SitOrSquat. Really, you can look this up; it still exists.

It was made for people living in or visiting New York City. What it did was rather genius. It told you where you could find a restroom in New York City whenever nature called.

When I first saw this, I remember thinking, "That is so much better than an advertisement," because what they created actually helped me as a New Yorker. I lived there for many years, and even I could never find a bathroom in the city. No one could (and it actually hasn't changed much, since public bathrooms are still few and far between there). Five or ten years ago, if you needed to, um, go in New York City, you went into Starbucks, Crate & Barrel, Barnes & Noble or some department store.

Here was a mundane and rather unsightly product whose company created something extremely useful to people. And it was all because they were paying attention to consumers' needs. They might not have been listening to data at that time, but imagine the needs you could uncover today by simply paying attention to what your consumers say on social media.

In the next chapter, we'll explore the forms of data that you need to pay attention to, and why.

What You Heard in This Chapter

▣ The old way of brand building—one that many agencies still use today—relies a lot on intuition and very little on data or proof.

▣ Digitally savvy companies and agencies have the ability to see very deeply into consumer behavior and, consequently, the scientific side of the equation has become more important than the creative side.

▣ A listening-centric company can respond to consumer feedback that isn't even directly related to its brand, product, or service, thereby building even more credibility and rapport.

Try This

What is an example of a company that has offered a helpful service, maybe even in the form of an app, that's not directly related to what it sells but clearly speaks to a well-defined audience? How effective has it been in improving the brand's reputation?

PART TWO

GATHERING
DATA

———

WHAT IT REALLY
MEANS TO LISTEN

CHAPTER 5

WHAT DOES "DATA" MEAN TODAY, ANYWAY?

So far, we've looked in depth at the old way of building a brand as opposed to the new—and better—way: by becoming a company or agency that listens and responds to consumers.

To really be a listening-centric organization, you need to be wholly focused on trying to hear overt messages from your customer or prospect, as well as those messages that aren't so blatantly obvious.

I'm not talking about wiretapping people's phones or reading their email, by the way. Rather, it's listening for the clues, the signs, in the data: playing like Sherlock Holmes and being a bit of a detective.

It's all about getting curious, as we discussed in chapter 2.

This chapter, which is all about data, will either make you nervous or excited, depending on your point of view. I'm hoping for the latter.

Digital Data Sleuthing

At the digital media agency where I am right now, well before we run any sort of campaign, we sleuth for clues. For example, I'll go to some of our big media partners—like Google, Facebook, Twitter, LinkedIn and so forth—or I'll use data-analysis teams we have in house, and I'll start looking at people's online behavior. I can't see their names, but I can find groups of people who look like those I want to reach, and I can find them as code.

Isn't it comforting to know you're being reduced to a bunch of numbers? I'm actually kidding, because this data reveals a lot about who people are and what they want in life. It may seem hard to believe, but the algorithms can show a detailed view of people in the aggregate: everything from their demographic makeup, their economic data, to things they click on and follow, people they like, searches they conduct, things they say, even what's trending with them on any given day. You name it, and we can see it in aggregate.

And we can see not just overarching consumer data, but also the connections between customers, which leads to a more holistic understanding of their behavior.

So that's what I'm looking at: data, numbers, words. Of course, it doesn't make much sense if you look at it without an eye for understanding what it means. But with a little training, I can now see what these people are interested in, what they do, what they care about and what the group is saying, overall. I can't see what individual people are saying, but I can absolutely see what the masses that matter are saying. I can see how people have moved around through GPS: whether they've traveled in different countries, states, counties, smaller regions. Like an undercover camera, I can see where these masses of people are during the day. Not only that, I'm beginning to be able to understand the exact words they're using when they talk to their friends and family.

Again, all this data is aggregated—it's information en masse. But I can still spot trends, words, proper nouns and the context in which people are talking about topics, like if it's positive or negative.

As an important note here, we are talking about "non-personal information" in this aggregated data, which means we aren't seeing anything identifiable associated with individuals. No names, no email addresses, no phone numbers, nothing that would identify individual people.

What We Can See

So are you nervous or excited, at this point?

This is all new territory. The industry is just now starting to explore this area; even the most innovative agencies are still simply scratching the surface of this potential.

Now of course, everyone who's surfing the web can see comments, posts and tweets. That's public information for anyone who knows how to do basic research on social media platforms. You can go to those platforms right now and do some sleuthing (but finish reading this chapter first!).

Increasingly, though, we're able to see information that is sent to closed-off audiences: smaller groups within social networks. This information is accessible to some agencies but not in any "findable" way. In other words, we have no ability to figure out a person's name or where they live. The data is provided to us through media partners in huge chunks of massive amounts of numbers and letters. It's a way for us to gain insights into behavior, not to analyze a specific person's movements online.

Rules and Regulations

You're probably asking yourself, "JR, is this all above board and legal? What about regulations and laws?"

Valid concern, but let's not get too distracted by that, as I am not an expert in the regulation part.

In my opinion, however, regulation is a really good thing. In the digital realm, regulation often seems to start in Europe. For example, at the time that I'm writing this book, the EU is looking at Google to see if it has become a monopoly. And Google is no doubt looking at this, too—note the recent creation of the Google parent company, Alphabet. Surely increased regulation partially inspired that decision.

That's actually an interesting case, because even the way we are searching online has changed in just the past couple of years. We rarely type in the full address of a website anymore, but instead the browser itself is the search tool. We might just type in simple words to get to the websites we want, and that's now considered an Internet search. I can't remember the last time I actually typed 'www' into anything.

Today we have companies that exert great control over what we see on the Internet and have access to. Europe is looking at all of this, and specifically at Google. The European Commission have called for tougher regulation on Internet search, including suggesting breaking up Google as a solution to its dominance in Europe. What bothers them is the potential conflict in Google having a search practice and then, on the other hand, having offerings or affiliates that benefit from showing up at the top of search results. It appears to be a conflict of interest. But this is still to be determined as of this writing.

Thinking about Google in this context, we can also look back many years ago, when Microsoft was the company that people were quite concerned about. But regulators stepped in and shook things up for Microsoft, which allowed other companies—like Google—to jump into that digital space and thrive.

Another example that took both sides into account is the cookie notice implemented by the EU recently, which raises consumer awareness that they are being looked at and followed as a piece of data. People can opt out; they can click "no" and choose not to be "followed" this way. There are even more options coming, and more regulation, as well—for example, related to knowing when something isn't an editorial piece but advertising.

As much as there are regulators concerned about these topics, there are also many institutions and organizations keeping an eye on everything and making sure citizens' rights are not jeopardized or overlooked. I have confidence that things will stay balanced and fair. The people have spoken and continue to speak, and they're not going to let all of that power go without a fight.

Four Types of Data

So how do we define "data" in the listening context?

When we think of data, it's usually information that's generated in four different ways. One of those, as I just mentioned, is a cookie.

A cookie is like a little marker that allows you to be counted or recognized. This is why you might see an ad on a website that relates to something you saw on a previously visited website. Cookies help companies achieve this magic trick. Those cookies allow many data-related companies to learn about you, remember you, or even bid on you for their clients or client's clients. This can get pretty heady, but basically a lot of different types of digital advertising companies need to have access to data to understand if you are an important consumer to serve one of their ads to—thus, pay money to make sure you see their advertisements.

I should mention that cookies are not foolproof because they represent a specific computer and browser. Since more than one person can use the same computer and browser, the data may end up conflating users' activities. There is also regulation, especially in Europe, about how long a company can keep cookie-data stored—such as just for a few months—and then the data must be discarded.

There's also an ID that people have almost forgotten now, but it was actually really popular during the heyday of AOL and the early 2000s. That was email ID. People use email for many tasks, and now it's become a way to find and reconnect with people. It's so common, we don't even think about the fact that email hasn't been around all that long. It's now completely integrated into our culture and our daily life, and we use it a lot when signing up or signing into digital platforms and apps, for example. Your email address is a way for digital companies to know that you are the same person when you're interacting in various digital spaces.

Then, of course, social media platforms sprang into existence. The early ones were called "bulletin boards," but it really wasn't until Facebook launched in 2004 that these platforms really started to take off. When these became big and grew to include many different pages and online experiences, some of them began to split off. Meaning, their social section may be different from their messaging section, and they are now breaking their services into different apps and interfaces. But all of these platforms have an ID for each individual, called a "social ID."

A social ID acts a lot like a cookie. A social ID allows you to understand consumers as a number, as code, per platform. For instance, Facebook has a different social ID from Twitter. Social IDs have weaknesses, too, as they are associated with social media brands—and those brands want to create what we refer to as "walled gardens." Facebook, Google and Apple, for instance, all want you to stay within their universe and only use their services and apps. In doing so, your social ID becomes valuable to marketers, and those social media brands can connect advertisers to their audiences. They want to be the only place that people spend their time online because that makes their IDs more and more powerful. And of course, they don't give out these IDs or make them compatible with others; they just sell access to advertisers on their platforms.

The fourth type of ID is a mobile ID. I'm not referring to your phone number, either. I'm referring to an ID for the device itself that you don't see. Brands like Android and iOS are especially strong in this space.

All of these IDs—cookies, email, social IDs and mobile IDs— are, for the most part, not compatible with one another. With the exception of big players like Apple and Google, most agencies and brands need to go to other data companies to find a way to connect the dots. This is all very new, but for the next few years, compatibility among differing IDs and their data will be a real challenge.

But we can still get a lot of data to match up today, and this will only improve over time. We can already get access to large stockpiles of data to draw out insights—insights based on facts, not intuition.

Is Data Really Private?

Since we've been talking about regulation, let's think about the logic for a moment, and why the data is released to marketers and agencies in aggregated ways. I could say, for instance, that I want to know everyone in east London who likes mountain biking and art, who used to live in North Carolina but also lived in New York for fewer than 10 years. Do that, and you start to be able to build a filter that would pinpoint JR Little!

You could find anyone in the world, because we all have such unique experiences that you can simply ask enough questions and you'll find them. This is clearly illegal—and wrong.

In my opinion, regulation is good because in general, it allows for more companies to participate in this investigative process and, therefore, encourages more competition in the online space. That's how you get better results, better performance and better innovation on behalf of the consumer.

After all, Microsoft didn't really bloom until AOL didn't successfully merge with Time Warner. Facebook and Google didn't really start to come to fruition until there was regulation placed on Microsoft.

We can imagine that as regulation is also applied to players like Facebook and Google—Google in the search space and Facebook in the mobile space (mobile because many people enjoy their Facebook experience through their phones)—there will be new players emerging: businesses and networks offering consumers something unique and useful.

And regulation is definitely good for agencies because it makes them—I should say "us"—relevant. If your clients need to work with five, 10 or 15 different companies to get data to analyze, it's not efficient for them to do it themselves. At the very least, they need advice on who to work with and how to work with them, which makes agencies useful in this process. If a lack of regulation allowed them to go to one source, or if they could find all the data themselves, agencies would lose their relevancy.

Insights and Connections

Of course, data has always equaled information from which we can draw insights. That's nothing new. But the data we get from digital and social is definitely new. It's richer ad infinitum.

You may have heard the phrase "the Internet of things." As more things in our world get Internet capabilities, then that's more things sending signals back to a server somewhere in the world, and more things capturing and reporting data.

That's what I mean by "digital" data—anything generated from people's usage of the Internet, which could be search results or people's movements through different websites. It could be trends on what they're writing about, or the content of their blog posts. It could be their geolocation, because that can be seen if they have GPS turned on. It could be anything related to the experience that they—we—have on the Internet each day.

Most people understand that somehow, somewhere advertisers are using technology and IDs to follow them around the web, but they don't fully understand, or care about, the nuances. In fact, all major websites use ad serving technology in their architecture that allows many digital advertising companies to recognize a cookie ID from a user's browser when the user visits a website. This is how advertisers decide which digital ads are served to people. A company with great ad inventory spots the cookie ID when it enters their system and they serves and ad based on various attributes that can be seen or deduced from the cookie.

I am oversimplifying this process, but the point is, a lot of players are gathering data with every movement we make online. For example, AOL has its code on a huge volume of websites, so when a person goes to different sites during a day, AOL adds a notifier to the cookie each time. Then—and they do this with millions of people—they can start to see patterns, which illustrate where there are opportunities to deliver something the consumer might want: opportunities to sell something or for being more overt and targeted in their messaging.

While we as individual consumers look at a website and see words, imagery or video, there is a layer of numbers, tags and code that is all connected to it. It's like a spider web of synapses that fire depending on how we move around the Internet.

It's all interconnected, and it's all reporting back to whomever is listening: what humans are doing, what movements are taking place. It's this same logic that allows websites to tell you what's trending right now or what's been most popular. To a lesser degree, this is why Amazon and Netflix are so good at what they do. They are built to understand you, if you will, so that when you sign on, they already have a sense of what your particular ID tends to like. Therefore, it gives your ID the sorts of things you're most likely to embrace.

Decisions, Decisions

What is spinning out from this? Something pretty interesting.

The data reporting and responsiveness by companies is getting so intelligent, that people don't need to work so hard to make decisions anymore. This is still an area where there's great opportunity, of course, but going back to my running shoe example, I don't have to look too hard to find what would suit me. Many of the different websites I visit probably already have a sense that I'm an active person, that I'm a certain age, that I have a certain lifestyle. They probably even have an idea of the type of foods I like. A shoe company has already done this kind of research; it has put the technical infrastructure in place so that it can start to recognize me and serve me ads, imagery, videos and such within the places I spend my time online.

Here's the important point: Perhaps none of the places I visit will have been a running shoe comparison-type website. By the time I actually land on a shopping website, the first thing I see is the brand that knows that I'm likely to choose it. It's the brand that knows most of my friends like it, and the brand that knows most of its consumers are like me.

Why? Because it's a "listening brand." It's literally getting to know me.

These listening brands understand that many of their consumers aren't finding them or experiencing them within category websites—like running shoe websites. The wise brands are trying to become more relevant to the cultural groups that relate to their products.

Another example: I could be looking at a gluten-free cooking website, and that website could be sponsored by Nike. Ding! There I am again, seeing Nike. I could be following my favorite Instagram celebrity who focuses on cosmopolitan workouts—and it could be sponsored by Nike. Ding! Ding!

Nike may know that people who like a certain pop artist on Spotify have also been highly likely to buy or like their shoes. Therefore, they can safely and factually—that's the important bit, actually—assume that the culture that likes that artist will also resonate with their product. And they could sell me their shoe. Ding! Ding! Ding!

It's those types of connections that intuition could not possibly make or prove. Because unlike intuition, these connections are actually provable: they are gleaned from online digital data.

In the very near future—because it's just beginning now—we will start to analyze commentary and imagery, as well. It's not quite here yet, but we'll talk about it because it's definitely heading our way. Here's a sneak peek, with more to come in a later chapter.

Commentary simply refers to anything people write online: blog posts or comments about a post, for instance, but basically anywhere they have typed words into a domain online. Those words can be pulled together and looked at as pieces of data associated with IDs. That's what's known as "commentary analysis."

Put all of this together, and you have the makings of a listening-centric company: a company that has access to—either on its own or through partnering with agencies—aggregated data that replaces the iffy intuition of the recent past with factual information.

In the next chapter, which is a shorty but a goodie, I'll provide two definitions that can help you to understand this listening ability with even more clarity.

What You Heard in This Chapter

- The term "data" in this listening context includes everything we do online—from clicking on things to writing things. We see this information because specific types of IDs can help us connect the dots.

- Not only does the consumer data start to paint a picture, but the connections between customers is what really leads to a more holistic understanding of their culture and needs.

- Regulation is good for everyone because it promotes best practices, privacy protection and helpful competition.

Try This

How have you seen this type of listening in action as you explore your own interests online? What types of data are companies putting together to form a clearer picture of what you're interested in?

CHAPTER 6

A NEW VOCABULARY FOR LISTENING

In this brief chapter, I'll introduce two phrases I've coined that help to describe the type of data-based listening we've been talking about: "macro listening" and "micro listening."

Macro Listening

I use the term "macro listening" to describe the activity of experts looking at code when they are trying to find small nuances that yield a big impact: the not-so-obvious connections between a brand and something else of significance.

For example, let's say that I'm a company trying to sell dog food. I can look at many different people who have dogs who appear to be the type of consumer I think I want to reach. I can also look at other things they might be interested in or feel strongly about. This could be everything from mountain biking to drinking beer, to loving pop music, to enjoying fashion, hiking, rock climbing and swimming.

If I keep digging, I will be able to see which one of those things is connected most closely to dogs. For instance, I might learn that the people who love mountain biking and hiking also really love to do those activities with their dog. Then I can start to envision offers, products, communications or experiences for those consumers. I might create something for them, like an article that says, "Here are the top 10 dog-friendly hiking trails in the country, so you and your best friend can enjoy the outdoors." And of course, I'll say that this message is sponsored by my dog food company.

You've already seen this type of communication in action, I'm sure. The best companies are the ones that are taking the data and using it in a measurable and very specific way. By reviewing the data so closely, they can see the scale of their audience: how many there are, who they are and what they tend to like. And most importantly, they are able to be helpful to consumers. As we've already seen, any interaction a company has with a consumer today should err on the side of being helpful as opposed to brandishing traditional overt "messaging."

The best advertising is no longer related to someone's hard-to-define intuition. A company's moves are—or should be—based on facts and data first, and the creativity part comes afterward.

By engaging in macro listening, I can start to see how disparate bits of information—insights, really—can be pulled together to build experiences that will appeal to consumers. I call this "macro listening" because you are listening to a large volume of data to spot the insights that inspire scalable opportunities—tactics that a lot of consumers will benefit from.

But it's the tiny, almost un-hearable things in that big data that need to be strung together: subtleties that you may not be accustomed to spotting.

This is all pretty new, so let me explain this type of listening activity with another example.

If you were talking to someone at a party and you were trying to figure out if they love dogs, and they said, "I love red wine, travel, hiking, mountain biking and pop music," none of that clearly tells you that they love dogs.

But online, you absolutely can see that that same person loves dogs. That's the macro listening part. You can see that they've visited websites related to dogs, or you can see that they've searched for dog-related items or that they often post pictures of or talk about dogs.

It takes time and it also takes very skilled people to do this type of listening, because despite what all the movies about artificial intelligence would have you believe, computers aren't there yet. They are still just machines that run on software. A human being has to know how to ask the software the right questions to find these sorts of aggregated, big-scale results.

That's what "macro listening" is, and it takes teams of people doing nothing but this kind of research to make it usable.

Let me give you another example. You work for an automobile company, and you need to sell a new car that is small, very low priced, void of many features and with a small engine size—it's just a simple car to get from point A to B and priced so that people with a low income can afford to lease it. So you decide to target young people with a lower income, as this would make an ideal first car.

As you start to look at the people searching for this type of car, however, you notice that many of them are not low-income young people, but many are actually older men and women from high-income households. You dig further, and what you find is that those people own two or more cars.

You dig further, looking at the sites they visit and the types of things they say and believe. What you start to understand is that these people use the smaller car for running errands, like getting groceries, or one of them uses it as a work commuter car only, whereas their more luxurious car is for the weekends and going out to dinner. This means that you now have the potential to sell this car to two audiences: the lower-income young people as a first car, as well as the older, wealthier people as a "grocery getter."

Micro Listening

"Micro listening," on the other hand, applies to a type of

listening that requires less data, or we might say fewer layers of data. It's a more overt type of listening.

Sounds simpler, right? Well, maybe not...

The potential problem with this kind of listening is that you need even more people to execute it, ironically. People are listening to the obvious things that data is telling them. For example, maybe someone has used your hashtag or your handle today, or perhaps your company is trending in social media, you're getting extremely high search results, or someone posted on one of your social pages. These are obvious findings from micro listening.

But first, you need people in place to listen for those sorts of things and then second, to act accordingly—and it often has to be done quickly, more nimbly than you might expect, which is why this type of listening requires more people and organization to execute.

Remember the mobile carrier case we talked about earlier in the book? That's what I mean by micro listening.

"Macro listening" is more about the long-term impact of the data, its implications and what you do with it. "Micro listening" is more about, "What can we do right in the moment to respond to and reach consumers?"

So what happens if you don't have someone on the team (or preferably several people on the team) engaging in micro listening? I'll give you a simple example.

Let's say I go to a Hilton hotel and have a horrible experience. I write a scathing review, and somehow that scathing review makes it to the top of the search results. Suddenly, when thousands of people search for Hilton they see the bad review I've written—and I've damaged the business in the short term.

If someone at Hilton were engaging in micro listening, they could respond quickly by contacting me directly via the platform on which I wrote the bad review. They could potentially ask me what they could do to ameliorate the situation and inquire if I would remove the review if I became satisfied that everything was settled well.

Perhaps behind the word "Hilton," the second and third most common words typed into search are "horrible" and "service." You have people trained to look for those things to make sure your business isn't in jeopardy.

Micro listening is not just a way to protect a business. It's also a way to seize opportunity.

For example, shortly before I began writing this book, the United States Supreme Court ruled gay marriage constitutional. What happened online? You probably witnessed it, yourself. Many brands jumped on the bandwagon and started using rainbows and positive slogans about marriage equality.

This type of reaction seems like business as usual to some degree now, but they were only able to do that because they have people paying attention to current events who have authority to speak on behalf of the company.

On the one hand, they're listening to the themes and things that might relate to their consumers. And on the other hand, they have people who can respond with something that benefits their reputation with those consumers. That's micro listening in action.

Both types of listening are really crucial in marketing today. What type of infrastructure does all of this listening require? That's what we'll talk about in the next chapter.

What You Heard in This Chapter

- The term "macro listening" describes the goal of trying to find small nuances in vast amounts of data that can yield a big, positive impact on business.

- "Micro listening," on the other hand, is looking for easier-to-spot clues—like consumers' posts or comments with hashtags and handles—but requires a super-responsive team to react in the moment to customers' conversations.

- The key to effective micro listening is having a team with the authority to act, or easy access to getting that authority from higher-ups.

Try This

Do a search on one of the major social platforms for a hashtag you're interested in. What trends can you see simply from looking at people's comments? If you were a company looking at these results, what action could you take that relates to something happening in the moment? What brands should be a part of the hashtag content you searched?

CHAPTER 7

CHANGE...OR ELSE

As we've just seen in the previous chapter, having both macro and micro listening infrastructures in place is what companies need, and they need to have it sooner rather than later. But I have to tell you, it's also the most challenging aspect of this new paradigm. It's an obvious but important point that big data and social buzz have no meaning if you don't have an infrastructure in place that will allow you to listen to it and, ultimately, act on it.

I know that change can be difficult, especially for large companies. However, this is one of those times when I don't believe they have a choice but to change their infrastructures and set up new teams.

We already have companies—even smaller companies—that are very digital savvy, and they're growing at a meteoric pace. They are disrupting established models, and that's going to continue to happen in every single business category, especially if the bigger players don't become savvier along-side the smaller ones.

Disruptive Data

Since we were just using Hilton as an example in the previous chapter, let's talk for a quick second about hotels and what has happened in that business category, all due to expert listening.

There used to be just one primary option for vacationing or business travel. If you went to another city and needed a place to stay, you had to find a hotel room, and all the somewhat nice hotels were generally the same, especially in regards to price.

But now, of course, we have Airbnb. Do we ever have Airbnb! Talk about a disruption. Airbnb was born out of a great consumer need—more flexibility in travel and, in return, additional income for those renting out their space. The company is leveraging social media and making things easier for their users to find, secure and enjoy a place to stay, almost anywhere in the world. During its first years, Airbnb's social practices were stellar, using an ongoing conversation to put people at ease when going to stay at a stranger's place. Today, its entire infrastructure depends on people having thorough profiles and recommending places to stay. Everything about Airbnb is helpful.

Another example of disruption because of listening to data: Netflix. It's amazing, the vision they had when they first started—mailing DVDs to people instead of making them go into a video rental store because they had the foresight to realize that brick-and-mortar stores would be absolutely useless when people started streaming video. Even when they didn't have the technology in place to stream, they relied on their mailing of DVDs to build recognition and get an infrastructure in place. Then when streaming became a real thing, they were the best positioned to benefit. Pure disruption over time, and pure genius.

But what's even more amazing now is how cleverly they use listening technology to keep their consumers engaged. They have the capabilities to see what people stream most often and, as a result, can get more of the content or even make it themselves, e.g. "House of Cards" and "Orange is the New Black." They also use the recognition of a user's ID to ensure that they can almost always offer you something you'll like. They put apt choices right in front of your eyes based on what you watched last. And now they have opened up an entire streaming category, with Amazon, Hulu and HBO all offering such services. Even Amazon allows viewers to decide what they will pilot and commission. Talk about listening to your audiences!

On the contrary, if we look at the traditional TV model, we have to wait for certain times for shows to be broadcast, or we have to record programs to see what we want when it's more convenient for us. Or worse yet, we have to use the remote control to sift through many channels just hoping to find something we want to watch.

Why would we do that when we can go to Netflix, where

Netflix has done all the work for us even before we open their platform? That would be like TV knowing what you wanted to watch before you clicked the "power" button on the remote.

Those are two of many examples of brands that have listening—or we could say helpfulness—at their core. There are other brands that are getting better at listening that have more of the traditional brick-and-mortar infrastructure.

For example, we can look at a company like Red Bull: a company that fully understands that people are not looking for their product in the context of wanting a sweet-tasting, high-caffeine beverage. They're thinking of the relevancy of Red Bull to the culture in which their consumers live.

Remember, listening in this new way means paying attention to the cultural context of the consumer and then responding to that culture appropriately.

Red Bull has an attitude. A tone. A vibe that they're creating through everything they do. Its infrastructure is vast, and it's growing. For instance, the company—remember, it's a beverage company—has studios creating music, video and events, and they're doing that because they deeply understand the interests of their consumers in a cultural context, not just a category context.

(In actuality, many people who drink it would probably say Red Bull tastes really horrible! Wouldn't you agree?)

A Listening Infrastructure

So how does one form an infrastructure that can not only handle disruption, but even create it? And can companies build it on their own?

The simple answer to the second question is, probably not. Data listening is complex, and it can't be done well by just one party. Not even the big tech players can do it alone today. There are many ad tech, data and consulting companies to help in this area, and their capabilities are changing every day. Oracle can do some of it, Adobe can do some of it, Google can help with a lot, media agencies have capabilities, and so on. But there are some big buckets to become familiar with. These will at least help you understand the gibberish that you will find when learning more about the different companies out there. Let's look at what an effective infrastructure covers:

1. Warehousing and sources of data: We have already talked about data sources in previous chapters, with more to come. It's the places where those bits of information are being collected against unique IDs. There are many ways to collect and store data, and each company will have their unique way to do it. These sources must also consider local regulation, like cookie expiration. So the inflow of data must be a never-ending stream.

2. Managers and/or holders of data: Someone has to make sure the data is legit and then make sense of the gibberish, so data management companies take hard data—in a format that looks like random numbers and letters—and

make sense of it. They can also merge and find overlaps between different sets of data. Sometimes it takes more than one company to make sense of the data. Maybe they cross reference emails, or maybe they cross-reference with bank and credit card information; there is more than one way to connect the disparate dots to find the data representing real people.

3. Data visualization: Companies that are experts in data visualization build dashboards and interfaces where a human can look at a screen and make quick sense of the data. This is the place where charts, graphs, word clouds and such come into play. It may seem like a one-off project, but anyone who has run a web-based tool knows that they are always in need of adjustments and updates.

4. Agencies or clients/in-house staff: These are the people who will execute change initiatives and other actions based on what the data reveals.

It's important to note that some places can do more than one task, and some of the points break out even further; there is no absolute, as this space is still very nascent. The most important thing is to stay curious and use the above as a rough guide when interacting with data experts.

We'll discuss other types of data coming up soon, but let's look at the teams and players in a bit more detail here.

Your traditional chief marketing officer at a Fortune 500 company is unlikely to have been trained to listen to consumers in this new way. And the world that they grew up in didn't work this way, either. Most likely, they became CMO because they loved the art, the intuition, the creativity of messages projected toward consumers in the hopes of persuading and swaying those consumers. The ethos of a traditional chief marketing officer is actually the opposite of what they have to be doing today.

When I look back at my early career in branding, I was successful prior to all this change because I was good at the intuition and charisma part. But even back in 2007, I could feel a change coming. I could see that those abilities were becoming less important, and today, fact-based digital data isn't just a new thing, it's everything.

Now, you need a team of people at the ready, especially for the micro kind of data we talked about earlier. It's preferable that they be in close physical proximity to one another (although that's becoming less of an issue now) because they need to make decisions very, very quickly. This is not the slowpoke "branding model" I discussed earlier. The new team is working tightly together, and the idea of a CMO meeting with their team once a month or meeting with their agencies once a quarter is just ridiculous. Everything has to move much faster than that in this socially and digitally connected world.

As of my writing this book, the number of mobile smartphones is about to reach three billion. Three BILLION. How can teams who only meet once a month attempt to react appropriately to that much data? The answer is, they can't.

If we think again about the gay marriage decision of the

Supreme Court, for example, someone had to say, "Maybe our brand could be relevant and put out an image or gif. How could we show our support for the LGBT cause that relates to our brand?" Then, a team had to jump on that idea and execute on a concept—fast.

Here's another key point: People in these new data-listening positions either have to have the full authority to make decisions and act on them immediately, or they have to be able to get approval to do so very quickly so that it's still responsive and relates to the zeitgeist of what's happening in the moment. These teams need to be close—whether physically or virtually—to the decision makers and preferably have that authority, themselves. They all need to be working in synch.

You also need people who can play in Excel and spot patterns and anomalies: people with an eye for analyzing the macro data we talked about before.

A Different Skill Set

What else has changed with marketing teams? The people themselves have changed. Instead of needing charismatic, creative, intuitive sorts of people, you now need people who can understand and process data, who know how to play with it, how to interpret it: people who really value data and are curious about it.

Since there is no academic education or course that specifically teaches how to leverage data in the digital space, only people willing to experiment can bring the necessary value to, and take the lead on, these projects. As a result, it can be expensive to hire these individuals, and you'll find that unfortunately, there is a lack of liquidity in terms of talent, as well.

If you're the creative type, it's not impossible for you to make this move in your career. If you're curious, that's really all you need, which is a willingness to figure out things you don't yet understand. Trying to master the process of analyzing data is just a matter of being forever curious.

To be candid with you, there are parts of the listening process I don't enjoy. For example, I don't enjoy looking at numbers. I don't enjoy playing with numbers. (I don't enjoy washing dishes, either!) But the question is, do I have to do it to stay relevant and in the marketing game? The fact is, there are some things I have to do before I can get to the fun stuff. The same is true for you. Stay curious and get comfortable with a continual learning process.

This whole new idea of listening to the consumer and almost allowing the consumer to build a brand is really different from most CMOs' experience and comfort level. In the past few years, I've seen many of them struggle with this new way of seeing a brand. They're accustomed to writing creative briefs and making ads because this has been the thing to do for so many years.

They work so hard to make the perfect ad, the perfect "spot," and then they put it out there...and now they're confused as to why the campaign isn't more successful. I have heard them say that they don't understand why people aren't watching it, why people aren't sharing it, and they're quite perplexed.

At this point in our travels together, you could probably give them the reason: It's almost always because they started from what they want to say and where they wanted to say it, instead of what the consumers want to hear and where the consumers are.

I'll go into a deeper description of the new role of the CMO a bit later on, but suffice it to say that many still don't understand some of the basics of paid social media. Most of the time when something "viral" shows up in our social media feed, it's because someone paid for it to be there.

The human component in this new infrastructure is by far the most complex. It's retraining people who are used to doing things one way and basically turning their world upside down. But the new infrastructure depends on them.

In the next chapter, we'll examine the technology piece— arguably an easier part of being a listening brand. We'll also talk about "hyper-collaboration" among teams and the impact it can have.

What You Heard in This Chapter

- An effective listening infrastructure has four main components: sources and housing of data, managers or holders of data, some way to visualize the data, and an agency or people to execute initiatives.

- The way that marketing teams are formed and interact has to move toward a much more collaborative model, where people are in constant contact with one another. This means the people, themselves, need to change or the types of people a company hires need to be different from the old days.

- People in marketing today need to be open to continually learning and growing along with the changes in the digital world.

Try This

What parts of this new listening model cause you the most concern? Why? What's one small step in this data-driven direction that you could take right now despite your concerns?

CHAPTER 8

LISTENING TECHNOLOGY AND LISTENING TEAMS

In the previous chapter, I shared the four basic elements needed to create a listening infrastructure: sources of data, managers of data, visualization and people to execute data-driven initiatives.

Now we're going to talk about the technology piece in more depth—the one that tends to scare people who aren't used to talking about it. But that's what I'm here for, to take the fear factor out of it for you. We'll also discuss the role of the team in more detail.

Technology factors into all four of those basic parts listed above, which makes it crucial to get right.

Tech Specs

First things first: Before you start working with data, you need to know that there are legal restrictions that you must abide by: for example, regulations as to how long you can keep the data and the sort of information you can use. No agency should be keeping people's personal, private information. Those who do have that type of information need to understand the law very thoroughly. This personal, private information has to be treated with care and respect, and you must follow the law.

OK, now that I've shared that disclaimer, on the technical side, the first capability you need is a connection to the data sources, like to Google, Twitter, Facebook or data from your own digital channels and campaigns This access can be a direct line, or more likely you'll gain access in an aggregated way through a service that pulls this data together for you. In any case, what you get will just look like numbers, symbols and random words. You'll need help organizing the data and making sure it's legit and clean—no duplication.

What happens next? You'll need help visualizing the data, so you'll need visualization software: a system that makes all those numbers, symbols and words suddenly start to be interpretable for regular people—like you and me, and like marketers who don't also happen to be data scientists. And honestly, even data scientists can't really do anything meaningful with the data until it goes through a few layers of cleansing and formulas. Only then can they start to see if something significant has scaled or not, thus spotting insights.

That's really what we're all looking for: something that has scale, things that relate or correlate to one another. The way to see this clearly is through data visualization, an interface that is commonly called a "dashboard," that will allow you to create charts, graphs or groups of related words called "word clouds." In short, it's a way to see the prioritization of these data points.

It's at this stage that the creatively minded person can begin to spot opportunities.

Quick timeout here: Thinking back for a moment to branding circa 2007, when did the creative people come into the room in those days? At the beginning. We were supposed to create the "brand model" from which everything else followed. We did the focus groups and the surveys and so forth and compiled that information. And then we used that information—and a heavy dose of intuition—to craft the supposedly compelling message.

Today, the creative team comes in at a completely different time, with a completely different frame of mind and vision. These people can start to see what is trending by putting all the pieces together—and then you get your insights into what to do next. As a result, these insights will be more impactful from pulling together all these fragmented actions that have been brought together onto one screen. The data leads the creativity.

What follows that part of the process? Conversations within that integrated team that we talked about. But then they have to be able to jump back into the digital space and take action. For instance, they have to be permitted to say or create something on behalf of the brand, promote something by pushing a piece of content into the social media feeds of consumers, book an ad on a digital platform, or alter a search result in some way.

Bring In More Players

As I'm writing this chapter, it all looks simple—on paper. In practical terms, it can be quite challenging.

We've literally upended the creative marketing process here: brought in tons of data and asked people to change the way they've been doing things by allowing the consumer to be front and center in the decision-making process related to what messaging is used.

This isn't easy. It's complex, and it requires people of various skills and talents to do it all because the data landscape is too fragmented to be managed by one team. And it would be impossible to do all of that on your own. You can't bring all of this in house because you'd have to be investing significant funds constantly—because everything keeps changing. This process requires a network of different players, altogether spending hundreds of millions of dollars.

In terms of complexity, we've already mentioned several different forms of data. For example, Facebook uses one type of ID. Google uses a different type of ID. Already, you need some ability to figure out how to connect different IDs that don't relate to one another and aren't connected directly. It's not like Facebook and Google are going to suddenly line up all their data points and start to work together just to make things easier for marketers. If only!

So what's the answer? I'm not sure there is one distinct answer, but I do recommend working with another player in the technology field that can help you make these connections.

There is a company called Acxiom, for example, that takes the disparate, disconnected chunks of data from all the different platforms, and then they connect the dots. Acxiom (and companies like it) comes into the game way before the dashboard software. They are trying to get you good, reliable sources of data and then put all of that data together into something that suits your specific needs. Acxiom takes data sets—from Facebook and Twitter, for example—and tries to make sense of it depending on your goals. Axciom has a way to match data from across different social platforms, but it isn't infallible (see my comment about "walled gardens" earlier this book). There are other players in this space, like Oracle and Adobe with their own unique capabilities. Remember, it's still the Wild West out here, to a large degree.

The dashboard software then takes the data and presents it in viewable form. An example is a company called Tableau, which builds software that makes sense of the data. In the future, there may come a time when a single company can provide the data and also make sense of the data for you in a dashboard. This is all so very new, it will change—and fast. The state of play as I'm writing this book is that you have a separate company like Tableau build customized software to create an interface that intelligent and creative marketers can use. Everything is developed according to your company's specific needs.

The next player, of course, is the end user. It could be the company—the brand—itself, or it could be an agency acting on behalf of the company, such as what I do. Finding people who can do this type of work is a challenge in and of itself. It already takes a certain type of person who is going to be interested in code and data, but then they have to turn it into something that a more strategic or creative person can understand. You really have different layers of talent that ideally are in one person: a lateral-thinking person, in that they can go very deep into the data, and then they can go very high into the creative interpretation of the insights you can get from the data. Honestly, there's a talent void here—at least right now.

Some companies are exploring doing this work themselves, but historically this doesn't work very well. For instance, companies have tried to take all of their advertising in house, and it's not very effective because they lose the pace of change. They can't keep up.

The reason an agency can adapt to change more quickly is because when agencies are working with many different clients, they're learning from each of those clients. They are able to see how what they're doing on behalf of an automotive company could benefit a technology company's brand. When a client takes all of this in-house, they're not able to see the breadth of the landscape, and they quickly fall behind.

If I had to describe this new listening-centric setup, I might say that it's "hyper-collaborative." The old way, you could always ask the same sequence of questions about a brand in focus groups—no matter what the brand was, really. It was almost like an assembly line. Now, when you're working with disparate pieces of data that are "talking" to you, you have to ask different questions. You can't follow the same old, same old "brand model" every time.

To be fair, there is sort of a regular sequence: Determine your audience, and see what they're doing online. This would include what they're talking about, what their interests and affiliations are, what their passions are. Then you act on what you see.

The thing is, though, unlike the old days, this new way of listening, deciphering and acting means that there are hundreds of opportunities to connect with consumers. And you don't know what to do until you see what the data says.

To avoid mistakes, you don't want to start creating something before you have a pretty good sense that it will work. For example, you might go into the dashboard and think all you need to do is make a TV ad. But the data might reveal that actually, you need to create an entirely new service, or you need to fix something at one of your retail locations.

An interesting example I heard recently was something Volvo did. Now obviously, Volvo designs and produces vehicles. But the company just developed body paint for bicyclists. It's a type of spray paint that you can apply to your body and clothing, and to the naked eye it isn't visible. When the lights on a car shine on the paint, however, it makes the bicyclist highly visible in the dark.

This product might seem really odd, considering Volvo sells vehicles and in some ways, bicycles are the "anti-car." Some of our urban centers are becoming more crowded, though, and major cities like New York and London have bike-share programs now. Unfortunately, a lot of people are getting hurt or even killed because the roads aren't safe enough for bicyclists.

Volvo created this safety body paint because it meets a need the company heard through listening to data, and it also aligns with the company's overall message of safety. The safety of human life comes first, no matter if it's inside a car or on a bicycle. This action had nothing to do with running a TV or magazine ad. It was just Volvo doing something useful. Sure enough, people talked about it and said great things about it on social media. Now, it is considered award-worthy work.

Today, it's not even about trying to figure out what to say, but it's about responding to the needs of people—no matter what those needs might be.

Even if it's just to be entertained for a few minutes while waiting in a line, riding the subway or sitting in a lobby.

The Cookie That Roared

Remember the Super Bowl XLVII in New Orleans in 2013?

Something happened during that contest that really got the advertising and marketing world's attention.

It was the actions of...a cookie.

Not the data marker ID kind. The Oreo kind.

The team behind Oreo was ready and waiting for the right moment to say something pertinent to the Super Bowl conversation. They were probably working in close proximity, looking for opportunities during the Super Bowl where they could talk about their brand. Maybe they could send a message after a touchdown or during the halftime show, for instance. They were looking for chances to be relevant.

How could they do this? They had the listening infrastructure in place. They had the teams of the right people in place. And someone on that team had the authority to act. There may have been a designer, plus someone creative with words, and they clearly had someone who knew how to execute quickly in the digital space.

Because they were prepared, they could respond to something that happened in real time.

And then, the power went out in the football stadium.

Oreo responded, and people listened.

Or I should say, Oreo listened, responded and created quite a stir on Twitter. Because what else were people going to do when the lights went out on the Super Bowl except turn to social media?

Oreo's tweet, "You can still dunk in the dark," made headlines. It was retweeted thousands of times and became a sensation.

Looking at this today, it seems a little bit ridiculous. What do Oreos have to do with a power outage? Or football? You don't eat Oreos in the dark (generally!).

But this was really the first big example of a company reacting to an event in real time. They got a lot of attention because of how cleverly they were able to use something happening in the moment to benefit their brand.

Using the vocabulary from this book, the Oreo tweet is an example of micro listening. They had people in place who were listening to things happening in social spaces, and they were able to respond quickly. It probably didn't have an enormous immediate business impact, but it definitely benefited their reputation. People are still talking about it (including me).

Just to explain what the macro listening angle would have been, if the people representing Oreo had been looking at different pieces of data, they might have seen that people were buying their cookies around the time of the Super Bowl. Or perhaps by analyzing data even more closely, they realized that Oreo is one of people's favorite snack foods to enjoy while watching professional football.

That "dunk in the dark" campaign was a great success. That's what I might call "easy micro listening." It's achievable. It can be done on a small scale, where you simply listen to the people in your direct circles and put something out that captures the moment and is relevant and a bit delightful.

But that was 2013, and things have changed a lot since then. Now, people are starting to get turned off by these sorts of responses by companies. It's getting a bit played out. This sort of quick reaction play is becoming an overcrowded field and, as a result, people are rather bored by it. And honestly, it's a light use of data. It's not the type of data usage that will revolutionize a business or build a business' long-term future.

The Time is Now

As we've seen, there is always something new coming along, and fast. Right now, many companies are posting cute little pictures that relate to the theme of the day. Maybe they'll start to move into video or into a completely different interface, like Snapchat. The idea itself will continue, but the tools people are using will change, certainly.

Not to put too fine a point on all of this, but companies that haven't even jumped into this easy bit of micro listening are really behind. And if it's all they've done, they're still behind. Way behind.

Many companies and agencies simply aren't making the shift, or they're not making the shift fast enough. They don't believe that this is the direction in which they have to go. While other companies and agencies are using the right words, but have little understand of what they are talking about; they are appropriating the word 'data'.

Shortly before beginning to write this book, I attended the Cannes Lions International Festival of Creativity, and I saw agencies doing this very thing, unfortunately. They would stand on the stage and say, "We used data to come up with this amazing insight, which led us to building this beautiful 15-second ad."

And I'm sitting there thinking, "This isn't what listening to data is for. It's not the right way to use it."

It's a twisting of this idea of listening to data, and it's not helpful to an agency's clients or to companies. But this is what the advertising and marketing industry, specifically those "Mad Men" people, have always done so well. They have used their charisma and their people skills to be persuasive to their clients, and then they've turned their skills into persuasive messaging.

That's what many of them are still doing, even with all the data that's available to them. This kind of appropriation will leave these people in the dust. They'll be far less important than they were before—irrelevant, even.

In a way, these agencies, in particular, are using this new data and retrofitting it to do what they want to do, and not what the consumer wants to do. Whether it's an agency doing it or a company doing it, it's a disservice to everyone. There is no possible outcome other than damage to the companies, because these practices will stall them and leave leadership in place who don't truly appreciate what data can do for their business.

This whole data-listening movement that I've been observing, and that I encourage people to enter as quickly as possible, is already having big consequences within the advertising industry.

For example, I recently discovered that one of the branding agencies that I was very familiar with is just a shadow of its former self, slashing 50 percent of its staff over the past six years and now on the verge of closing entirely. The reason? They don't have the right talent in place.

That's why is so important to change the underlying infrastructure. Doing so will "future proof" an organization. If you don't have people in place who are curious about data, who understand data and enjoy looking at it, and then you aren't connected to the sources of data, you are writing your own exit strategy.

What's the moral of the story? Engage in listening by having the right technology and teams to help you, and use what you find in the right way: to connect with and be helpful to consumers in a way that they can relate to. Remember who's holding the megaphone.

It's important to be able to distinguish a couple of different types of data from each other so that you really know what you're seeing. Let's do that in the next chapter.

What You Heard in This Chapter

▣ Getting the technology piece right is as crucial as getting the right team in place. Don't go it alone.

▣ The creativity part of the marketing process now comes last, not first—for a very good reason. You're almost guaranteed a good result when you follow the data's implications and serve the consumer, instead of using data to develop what you think is the "perfect" ad.

▣ Oreo's tweet during the Super Bowl was an early indicator of the power of listening to data and having an infrastructure in place that allows a company to respond to events in real time.

Try This

What objections might a company have toward moving toward this listening-centric model? What would you say to them to overcome those objections?

ANALOG LIFESTYLE DATA VS. DIGITAL DATA

To further clarify some terminology that's important to this discussion, I'd like to make a distinction between data. These are not formal words that people use, but they help you to decipher what someone is really talking about when someone drops the data word in a conversation. I'd like to distinguish between "analog lifestyle data" and "digital data." Whenever you're talking about understanding consumers through reviewing data, you'll likely want to make sure the context is clear.

Analog Lifestyle Data

"Analog lifestyle data" means the information that is gained through people's self-reporting activities, such as via a questionnaire, an interview and/or a focus group. People tell you how they live their life or what they do, as opposed to us looking at the facts of their life or what they do through digital data. Sure, someone can answer an interview online, but this is still considered analog—unless, of course, you are clever enough to get a digital ID from them, and then you compare their analog answers to their actual digital behavior. In that case, you are looking at both analog data and digital data and comparing them.

Analog is essentially synonymous with traditional consumer/marketing research that companies have always done. There are two types of analog data. Quantitative (binary data) is when a researcher uses a statistically significant sample size to uncover trends; these are often surveys. Quantitative data tends to need a statistically significant sample, although there can still be error in both choosing the questions you ask, and leaving out important questions you may not know to ask.

Qualitative (anecdotes) is when a researcher attempts to garner testimonies by questioning a broad representation of their audience while making them comfortable enough to talk openly; these tend to be one-on-one interviews and focus groups. It does not need to be a statistically significant sample, but it does need to be broad enough to represent all the differing types of people in your audience. Clearly, assumptions must be made in order to get this sample.

As we have discussed—and this is important to reiterate—how people choose to present themselves to you is not always the reality. In a way, when you conduct this type of research you have to trust that people are being accurate and authentic, and that they're remembering and considering everything they say and do.

But whether they realize it or not, these people are always putting a filter on what they say. Meaning, there's almost always a difference between what the honest answer is, and the answer they want to provide to you.

There's also an element of what's on top of their mind—what comes to mind first when they see a question you're asking. The subconscious mind filters thoughts that might make them uncomfortable, as well, so you rarely hear the truth in these situations.

The problem is, even if their responses were 100 percent truthful, this information is only letting you see a tiny fraction of what a person actually does, or what they feel or believe. Between what they *actually* do every day and what they *say* they do every day, there's a lot of ambiguity. Nothing is black and white. Even gray is a shade too bright for this kind of information.

Oftentimes, people think sample size makes a huge difference, but honestly, I'm not so sure, especially not in qualitative. The responses are still being prompted by the questions that the survey or interviewer is considering—not the actual behavior of the people who are providing the answers. Back in the day, when I was conducting a lot of one-on-one interviews and focus groups, we could see patterns in responses from about 15 interviews or three groups. And with regards to quantitative data, if the survey design is flawed, the entire output will be skewed—thus you may miss an important insight because you didn't ask the right questions.

Do you see the difference here? At this point in our discussion, it's really important that you do. So if you have any questions, please feel free to stop right here and go back a chapter or two and come back to meet me right here in this spot.

Because when you collect this analog lifestyle data, you're already setting up the type of answers you're going to get because of the type of questions you're asking. This method leaves out the beauty of happenstance, of serendipity. It leaves out the "Eureka!" moments that can happen when you're looking at digital data—where you'll see information emerge, when you never would have thought to investigate a particular area of inquiry before.

By the time you've developed a questionnaire or a discussion guide for a focus group, you've already created a hypothesis. Even if you think you haven't, even if you believe you're being thoroughly objective, you still have created a bias in some way. There's a constraint on the conversation, even if it's as simple as a time constraint.

For example, someone may be answering a questionnaire online, and there are only 50 questions. Perhaps the focus group lasts only two hours, or a one-to-one interview is only allotted 45 minutes, so you have to start these conversations with some hypotheses in order to fit everything into the time you have available to you.

The difference with data is that you look at many, many hours of online commentary and behavior. You look for anomalies, which can turn into those "Eureka!" moments, like certain dog lovers also being huge fans of hiking and microbreweries.

These days, I don't even consider a statistically significant sample size in quantitative or a broad representation in qualitative as enough analog lifestyle data to lead me to see trends. But this is what most companies still do.

Are there ways to truly scale this type of research? Yes. Maybe you ask a large number of people to take an online survey, document their day via video or talk to you on Skype. But it's still self-reporting.

Going back to my university class where I watched the young students and documented what they did in preschool, data allows us to engage in proper anthropology: look at the facts for what they are, and see which how those facts create patterns and anomalies.

It's observing. It's watching. It's listening.

Analog lifestyle data might be asking people how they spend their time, what TV channels they watch, what websites they visit, their favorite pastime, foods, vacation spots. All in all, this reporting is not very reliable. If you ask enough people, the data can start to become reliable. But when you think of marketing, we're ultimately trying to get people to change their thinking and, therefore, their behavior—all to benefit our business. Maybe that action is to buy our product or sign up for our services.

What this really means is that we should be getting to know these people deeply.

We should be trying to understand how they think and the subconscious motivations behind their thinking.

It's extremely difficult to do this through any type of self-reporting resource. Think about when you talk to another person. How much can you really get to know them through what they say to you? It's almost never the reality of what's happening inside their minds. Dating and marriage is a key example: it takes a lot of time to truly understand human behavior in an analog way. Actions speak louder than words, as they say.

That's why this sort of research can only help us so much. We still need to do this type of research, but there's so much more we could be listening for. Now, we have the resources to do that.

Patterns of Digital Data

Before we talk more about patterns of digital data, I'd like to mention that companies still need to collect analog lifestyle data—but just not as extensively as they're accustomed to. And they should never rely on it to present an accurate picture of the consumer or as a sole source for sparking creative ideas. We are trying to deeply understand people's needs and wants, so we have to go much further. Fortunately, we can do this rather easily now.

As we've discussed, every person who uses the Internet or a mobile device has a unique ID associated with those activities. As a result, all of the things we do online can be strung together into patterns.

For example, because of cookies, you could literally see everything I did online on my laptop from the time I woke up until the time I went to sleep during the day. By looking at that sequence of activities, you can start to see how many people are doing similar things—or how significantly sized groups of people might be doing similar things.

What may happen is that by looking at these patterns, you start to develop sub-segments based on people's activities. Listening in this way is about observing these patterns and seeing where there are overlaps. Where do you have consistencies within large groups of people? Where do you have differences?

Here's a hypothetical example. You're a company that sells an ice cream product in the United States and also in the United Kingdom. Looking at patterns of data, you may find that on one day out of the month, the search behavior for this particular product was very active in the US South. You might ask yourself, "Why was that happening?" What you might find is that on that particular day, temperatures were quite high in the US. You see a correlation, and unless you were doing this type of listening, you would never gain this level of understanding. This is a very basic example of spotting a correlation, but it illustrates what we're talking about.

Perhaps you're a company that sells clothing, and you notice a surge in search results one day in the UK. When you look closer, you see that a popular celebrity was wearing an item of your company's clothing on a British late-night talk show. Then you also see that online purchases of this particular piece went up the next day, and that people started visiting your website, talking about it on social media or clicking on other websites that are tangentially related to your product, including third-party retailers. If you are listening acutely, you might want to do something within 24 hours to sell more of that item, get more stock or even try to leverage the popularity to sell other items.

With this type of listening, you're seeing what actually has an impact on purchasing behavior. You can confidently make statements such as the following:

- This particular celebrity influences the buying behavior of our customers.

- The people buying our product are older than we imagined and live in the suburbs.

- This late-night talk show reaches a large segment of our audience.

- This search engine is the one most of our consumers use.

- These phrases are most often used in their searches.

- Most of them are searching from this specific type of phone.

- Few people are searching from a desktop computer.

- They tend to own these specific types of devices in their house.

- When they're not buying directly from us, they tend to go to this other retailer's website.

- But after they went to the other retailer's site, most of those people didn't complete their purchase there and actually bought from a third website because the price was lower.

- They almost always share a picture of their purchase on this social media channel.

Do you see how these patterns start to emerge when you're listening in this way, as opposed to paying attention to analog lifestyle data that you collect via people's self-reporting? This type of data collection and analysis starts to produce very accurate results because it's not people reporting to you, with all the margin of error that's present there.

Here, there's no guesswork. It is a record of what actually happened. And this record is generated very quickly.

If you want to take it further, you can look at other actions these people have taken, which may or may not relate to your clothing. For example, if those same people who saw the clothing item being worn by the celebrity on TV then searched for it and purchased it, then we can look at where else they've been online, as well.

You might find out that they also really love Taylor Swift because they spend a lot of time looking at Taylor Swift content online. So what does that tell you, potentially? That you might want to explore associating your brand with Taylor Swift: advertising on her website, or connecting with her to see if she would be willing to talk about your brand in her social channels.

It's these overlaps and correlations that become apparent: patterns that are sometimes explainable and sometimes not. But they're there. They're proven through facts. That's the beauty of this online marketing world. There is no human error. It's simply reporting actual human behavior as it is.

Broken Patterns

Let's look at a really cool example, one that I can't talk about at any length because it's not my area of expertise, but I find it absolutely fascinating.

The Higgs boson study in Switzerland was a hugely expensive enterprise. They built this big collider under the ground, but most people really didn't understand what they were trying to accomplish. And how did they even know they had accomplished their goal?

The goal was to create something new: a particle that did not exist before.

The way they knew they achieved this goal was by looking at data. In actuality, the data looked like dots. The dots were gathered onto dashboard screens, day in and day out for a very long time.

One day, there was a dot that didn't fit in line with all the other dots.

That dot was the creation of new mass. Universe explained. Goal accomplished.

I'm seriously oversimplifying the study, but that is pretty much what happened—an anomaly happened in the data.

This listening that we're talking about is searching for patterns, for things that make sense together. But it's also looking for the things that don't make sense. It's asking, "Where has the pattern been broken?"

You can apply this idea to anything that has to do with the interface between a human being and the digital world. That synapse, if you will, fires through the touch of a finger or the touch of a mouse click. That action creates a piece of data, every single time.

For example, you'll have data reporting to you when people visit your website. It will tell you where they're spending their time and how long they're spending time there—even by each page. You'll also see which page is the one they visit last before they leave the site, and their behaviors will start to show you why. This is some of the magic of Google analytics.

You'll ask questions like, "Where do they go next? Are they taking that action because they are satisfied or unsatisfied with our site?" Here's an example to share. Recently I was working on a large campaign for a client. We were hosting expensive events all over the country and needed people to go our website and sign up. We wanted them to sign up mostly so that we could get more data on them, but that's not the point of this story. The point is, they were not signing up.

When we looked at the data, we noticed that we were getting more signups from desktops than mobiles. Ding! We had a problem.

Then we noticed that a vast number of people were signing up from a type of mobile device that wasn't the biggest mobile player in that country. Thus, we were not getting signups from owners of a certain type of mobile device—the most popular mobile device in the country. Ding, ding! It seems our signup page might not be working well on certain types of mobile phones. So we looked further, made the changes, and things started working again.

Then, we noticed a lot of signups on one specific day—the same day that we ran a newspaper ad. Ding, ding, ding! Our consumers tended to sign in from a certain type of mobile device, and our newspaper ad on that day seemed to resonate with them more than anything else.

When we put all these insights or signals together, we start to see how we could improve the performance of our current and future campaigns. We look for signals of what worked, what signals impacted other signals and what signals are not firing at all. We try to see what led to what, and to what degree (some people refer to this as attribution modeling).

And this could go on and on. We could look at where our article ran, what was being said in that paper, what topics and celebrities they liked, what they were saying online, what other brands they followed, what music they listened to. You get the idea. Constantly digging for information out of curiosity.

In the best marketing firms today, these are the kinds of questions that are being asked day in and day out. Why? Because the guesswork—the intuition I talked about earlier—is taken out of the equation. It's not relevant. Only curiosity and fact are relevant.

There's an old saying about advertising that goes, "Fifty percent of my advertising spend is wasted. I just don't know which 50 percent it is."

That's not true anymore. Because today, we can absolutely see which 50 percent is wasted and the nuances of that waste. When we have a history of patterns, we can guess and predict what we should do with almost pinpoint accuracy.

I wish I could say that we are at a place today where we can trust data solely, but we aren't—although in time, we might be. Thus, there is still a role for both analog lifestyle data and digital data when forming insights.

The challenge with digital data is that it doesn't give the full picture just yet because much of our life online is as curated as answers to surveys and discussion guides can be. As a result, it can make it challenging for us in branding to understand *why* we are seeing what we're seeing.

I'll give you an example. With medical trials, where several small but very controlled groups are used, experiments are repeated again and again to see whether trends are correlated or causal. For instance, there were trials that saw a correlation between pregnant women who drank one glass of wine a week and higher IQs in children. What was really going on here? The group who drank in this way tended to be middle-class, well-educated women: these facts were more likely to drive the high IQ scores, not the wine.

I do believe that even when we get closer to a fully connected digital picture, we can still ask people questions that are difficult to infer via behavior digital data. The most powerful insights will happen when we bring analog and digital data together.

It reminds me of how I've seen ethnographic research conducted: observing and listening, yes, but then revisiting and asking people if they can explain their behavior to try to unpick the reasons for their decisions. Importantly, these ethnographers teach us that we cannot take things at face value. Everything we uncover provides another layer to assist us in our interpretation and analysis.

Are you ready to dive into the most exciting type of data of all? Then join me in the next chapter.

What You Heard in This Chapter

◙ Analog lifestyle data is the result of traditional consumer/ marketing research using a statistically significant sample size to uncover trends.

◙ Observing patterns of digital data allows you to look far deeper into consumer behavior, seeing overlaps and con- nections you wouldn't have thought to even ask about with traditional marketing research.

◙ When patterns are broken, those anomalies can create opportunities to improve or delight.

Try This

Here's an experiment for you that mimics what we're doing in the digital space. Go to a location that gets a lot of foot traffic—like real-world foot traffic—and spend 30 minutes sitting on a bench, observing people's behavior. What do you see? What do you hear? Listen and watch as an anthropologist would, just recording but not making judgments. Then look at your notes. What patterns or anomalies do you see? What behavior did you witness? Observing—or listening—with an open mind can present opportunities.

CHAPTER 10

LET'S GET SOCIAL

Social data may be the most exciting area of all when it comes to transforming into a listening brand. In fact, it might be the most important area, as the insights from social data are based on actual conversations and should be the foundation of our thinking and targeting.

Why should we target audiences if we don't know who they are, what they like and don't like, or even if they're interested in us at all? Today, we have the means to fish where we know the fish are—to go where we're wanted. And we also have the means to know why we are not wanted. Until now, that's been guesswork or we've been trying to get to it by asking questions and having people self-report: putting together the puzzle pieces.

We don't have to do that anymore. This new reality we're living in is extremely helpful when you have pressure to meet sales targets. You can sell to the people who love you and change what you're offering to the people who might grow to like you—and then avoid the people who don't like you at all.

It all means greater efficiency across every aspect of business.

↯ Fish where the fish are. Don't be the company that has a product to sell to a group of people that you've decided to target, but those aren't the people who are even talking about your product. You're missing a huge school of fish that are ready to bite your hook.

What is "Social Data"?

"Social data" refers to the data points created from social interactions in digital spaces. Every time someone writes a tweet, posts a comment on Facebook—whether they post it just to their friends or to everyone—and every time someone writes a comment on a Huffington Post article or a YouTube video, and so forth: all of this activity in these social spaces can be turned into data points. These data points can be used in association with those unique IDs that we talked about earlier.

In a way, we can consider these kinds of interactions—the ones that specifically reference a company by posting on their wall, for instance, or using a handle or hashtag—as direct messages to a company or brand. It's almost like the new email, in that it's how many consumers contact companies today.

So that's the first type of social data: direct messaging that uses a hashtag, handle or something like posts to the company's Facebook page.

In the chapter where I discussed regulations, I mentioned that people's privacy is protected by law. I want to reiterate that here, but I also need to say that there is a lot of data that is readily and easily accessible to marketers. An obvious example would be when someone uses a hashtag or handle, which creates an easy, visible link to a company or topic that's easy to find via search.

Increasingly, however, even words that aren't used as hashtags or handles can also be searched. Now we're getting into the other two types of social data: commentary analysis and sentiment analysis.

What They Say, What They Feel

Right now through social media partners, we can learn whether someone spoke about a brand—let's say a trail mix brand. That's the basic social data, which shows us references to this particular brand of snack.

Well, what else were they saying in that sentence? What else do they say often, and what exact words do they use?

At this point, if it's words that they have actually typed by their own hands (or spoken into their phone as a voice-to-text message), then chances are it's a topic that's top of mind. They're posting a comment for a reason. When the words start to have adjectives along with them, or emotional identifiers—like sad, happy, hate, love, awesome, amazing—then you're able to identify a sentiment as well as the commentary.

Talk about getting closer to deeply understanding the thoughts and feelings of a consumer!

The whole purpose of marketing is to change thinking and behavior. We're trying to persuade people to want our product, to think positively about our product and actually buy and consume our product. So the closer we can get to understanding what they think about and how they feel, the better we can be at persuading them—and the more we can be on their mind and part of their daily culture. This is why commentary analysis is so powerful.

Remember the whole discussion about understanding the cultural context of the consumer and your product? This is where it all converges.

In the trail mix example, we might see comments like, "This trail mix is so great. I ate the whole bag on the bus to work. I'm so addicted!" That tells us not only that they like the trail mix, but it also reveals how they consume it—in one sitting, and during their commute in a busy city location.

It tells us the words they use, and—bonus!—It might also tell us things like a certain brand of juice they drink while they're eating trail mix, the social media app they use the most, how many followers they have, what kind of work they do, how far they commute, etc. That information allows us to consider partnerships with other companies, or specific imagery we might want to use when we connect with them, because we're seeing the nuance in people's behavior instead of simply asking them to self report.

With all this data in front of us, we're beginning to form a clear picture of what these people are doing, how they're using the products and how we can leverage other aspects of their culture.

For example, if we see that a majority of our consumers have dogs, perhaps we want to do something nice for the dog-loving community, like support animal shelters. Going back to the trail mix example, instead of forming a partnership with the juice company (because we learned they love their trail mix and juice in the morning), maybe we want to buy a juice company or start producing juices and sell it ourselves. Social data can reveal business opportunities as well.

You start seeing all of this information—incredibly important and influential data—simply through people's patterns of clicking and moving around online. And you'd never see this if you were just doing interviews and asking people to fill out a questionnaire. It's not possible.

There are so many ways you can explore conversations, and it can take you in hundreds of different directions. When you get right down to it, it's really all about the dynamics of human relationships and behaviors. You can keep finding out more and more and more, ad infinitum. And that's the beauty of commentary and sentiment analyses. It all indicates the degree of positivity or negativity toward your brand within a sequence of words.

Commentary analysis is still done via consolidated, aggre-gated data. Right now, at least, you can't figure out what a specific person said—it's absolutely not possible. As for the future, who knows?

The next area that's going to measurable, in fact, is sentiment analysis. Right now, this area of data analysis is really new. But sooner rather than later, agencies and media compa-nies are going to start advising brands as to whether they're being spoken about positively or negatively in public—which is easy to find today—but also in private groups and other places that aren't currently accessible. Even emoticons in private posts will be turned into data points that help us understand a consumer's sentiment in relation to other things like our brand. As I write this, Facebook has rolled out a new way to comment on posts through many emoticons, they call these "reactions." This new rollout from Facebook is a clue to the role sentiment will play in our online lives.

Commentary and sentiment analysis can go much further than insights for your marketing, social media or content strategy. It can also be used for new product development and overall corporate strategy—if you're trying to reach investors, for example, and you want to know if people see you as a progressive (or not-so-progressive) company. This commentary and sentiment analysis can help with inventory management, as well. If, for instance, a lot of people in the US are talking about a product, but not many people in the UK are talking about a product, you might discover more quickly that you need more of that product in the US marketplace. Crisis control is another area where this type of analysis can come into play. As I'm writing this book, Volkswagen,

Skoda and Audi are in the public eye—and not in a good way. Social listening would be in their best interest right now and could tell them quite a bit from a crisis management point of view. So even though we've been talking about listening to commentary and sentiment in terms of brand building, it's not just for the chief marketing office in the boardroom. It's something everyone in that boardroom can use.

What's Coming Next?

In time, there will be image analysis, as well. We already have the technology for face recognition, and at some point in the near future we'll have the ability to understand the types of images people share. We'll be able to answer questions like these: What type of emotions is that image capturing? What objects are in the image? Are there people and/or animals in the image? What location is depicted? Do they look happy, sad, frustrated or excited when they're around our brand?

Just like with commentary and sentiment analyses, you'll be able to pick up on emotions through visual cues. It's all a form of language that is turned into data, and that data can be a powerful tool for marketers. Players like Google, Facebook and Blippar will help make this future a reality.

Most companies today are, at the very least, looking at simple social data: hashtags and such. When a person uses a hashtag or handle, they're really saying to the company, "I'm talking to you. It's up to you if you want to talk to me."

In essence, they're creating a link to your company by using the megaphone. It's in their hands, and they're the ones initiating the conversation. The smart companies have caught on and are receptive to direct and indirect messages, such as any time the consumer talks about something tangentially related to their brand.

As for sentiment analysis, we're right on the forefront, and it's starting to happen now through large social platforms like Facebook. Even though this type of analysis is just beginning, companies can still get an idea of positivity or negativity by the way people are using hashtags, for example; simply study the words that people use along with hashtags and handles that are somewhat related to your brand.

You can also use search results as a way to see relatively quickly how people feel about your brand. Are people searching for your brand within a negative, positive or neutral context? So even something as relatively simple as search terms can give you a sense of how people are experiencing your company.

Putting It Together

Before we leave this topic of social data, let's do a run-through of a complete example, so you can really see how this all works. We'll combine self-reported analog lifestyle data, patterns of digital data, social data and commentary and sentiment analysis.

Let's say you're a company selling doggie treats, and you want to more deeply understand your current and potential customers.

You have a sense of who your consumer is because you can review your sales data, for one thing. The treat you are selling is sort of pricey, so you also have an idea of what the consumer's socioeconomic status needs to be. And of course, you can look at self-reported market research, such as questionnaires and focus groups. This kind of information will tell you a little bit about them—some of the things they say they're interested in, what they do for fun, other brands of doggie treats they purchase or types of media they consume regularly.

What happens if you start looking at digital data patterns, in addition to this analog market research?

Well, you might be able to confirm some of what they've already told you via self-reporting. But you might also start to see some new information about what they're doing or what they're interested in—things you would never have thought to ask about because it didn't seem relevant to dog food. Looking at the data, you notice that certain interests are quite common among the consumers you're trying to reach.

Go deeper into this analysis, and you look at commentary. You might see that they're talking a lot about one of the interests you saw in the data patterns—the interest that had nothing to do with doggie treats. What's curious is that they're using similar vocabulary when they talk about dogs as they do when they talk about this other activity. And sometimes they're even talking about the dog inside the context of that activity.

Let's put a name to this aggregated consumer group. We'll call them "Jack." Clearly, Jack loves dogs because that was the prerequisite for even looking at Jack. Then you see that Jack likes hiking, beach travel, and eating gluten-free foods. What else does Jack like? He likes independent movies: documentaries, in particular. He also likes beer. We are starting to get a great sense of who Jack is and how he lives his day-to-day life—even where he tends to live.

Next, you start to consider how all of this data can help your business. You're trying to sell dog food and you want to be more relevant to Jack. You want Jack to like your company as much as he likes other things in his life. You want him to think about you, talk about you, build rapport with you and appreciate your brand. Yes, you are simply a dog food company, but you want to be on his mind when he thinks about feeding his pup. You want to be there consciously or unconsciously.

How could you use one of those other things that Jack loves to benefit your brand? Perhaps through commentary analysis, you figure out that Jack likes to take beach holidays where he can also go hiking. He brings his large-size adopted dog along, and he likes a cold beer to relax. We can also see that that cold beer makes him very, very happy. He loves to post pictures of himself with a beer in one hand and the other around his best buddy—Rufus, the mixed Labrador.

(Remember, "Jack" is a personality we've associated with aggregated data, not an individual person. And Rufus is a stand-in for dogs in general.)

You can begin to form some really tangible ideas. You could do something to help Jack find places where he can take his dog on holiday—places with great hiking trails that allow dogs. You could be on those hiking trails offering poop bags. You could print hiking tips on the back of your dog treats box. You could make an app with dog-friendly parks and pubs located by GPS and so on. The creativity flows once you have the data-based in hand.

Do you see how you start to play a role in Jack's life? You now have a purpose and can be helpful to him: providing him with something valuable that means a lot to him, culturally. And notice how we didn't just make a TV ad of some guy hiking and drinking a beer. Yes, that might be in the final marketing plan, but it wasn't our objective when we started digging into the data.

Suddenly, you're not just a company that makes and sells dog biscuits. Now, you're also a company that can show Jack some new places to take his dog on holiday, go hiking by the beach along with his dog, and enjoy a nearby microbrewery or pub. You are a company that cares deeply about the relationship between Jack and Rufus.

If you were Jack, would you pay attention to messaging like that? Absolutely. Chances are good that there will be a strong, positive association with your brand in Jack's mind.

You are becoming useful and meaningful to him—you are becoming a lifestyle brand.

The Real Goal: To Be Helpful

Think about what we've been talking about throughout this book. We've been referring to this idea of a listening brand. Why are you listening?

You're listening for the purpose of being helpful, useful—giving people something they haven't had before that also makes you compelling and different. You'll mean something to them, and ultimately, the goal is for them to think positively of your brand and talk positively about your brand to the other people in their life.

If this hypothetical doggie treat brand listens to self-reported data, to the patterns of digital data, and to commentary analysis, it's absolutely foolproof that they will find a way to be helpful to Jack. If we can do this with dog food, just imagine what we can do for selling tech devices, cars, human food and clothing.

You may be asking, "But what about traditional advertising, JR? Can't all of this listening be in service of that, as well?"

Yes, it can. But that's not the ambition, not at all.

Why? Because the role of trust has changed in society and, consequently, so has the role of the brand.

I truly believe that today, a brand's role is to be useful in serving a purpose. We cannot shout at people anymore. We cannot pick up the megaphone again and start blaring our message. It won't work, because we are talking about brand-savvy human beings, and now we have much better ways of seeing who they are and what they want. Why wouldn't a brand want to engage with people in this way? Don't be the last one left shouting.

Of course, people are needed to execute on these findings. In the next chapter, we'll examine who these people are: the essential qualities that make up a responsive, listening brand team.

What You Heard in This Chapter

- "Social data" refers to activity in social spaces that can be turned into data points, which can be used in association with unique IDs.

- Commentary and sentiment analyses are on the leading edge of listening to social data, with image analysis coming soon.

- Remember that the ultimate goal in listening to data is not to serve up the "perfect" ad, but to be helpful to the consumer.

Try This

Open up your favorite social media app on your phone. Have a look at the pictures being posted. What can you see by looking at the commentary under those pictures and even the sentiment within the commentary? What emotions are you are seeing? Does a brand have anything to do with the situation?

PART THREE

ACTING ON THE DATA

———

WHY LISTENING IS IMPORTANT BUT IMPLEMENTING IS MORE SO

CHAPTER 11

HOW DATA CAN BE USED TO BUILD MICRO TEAMS

As we have just seen in chapter 10, today's branding strategy is about building a company that isn't just selling, but is responding to the consumer on a very deep level. If you want someone to embrace what you offer, you need to resonate with them, and not simply talk *at* them (like the rock star presenter did at that conference I mentioned). This kind of connection means that brands have to use all different types of data in order to understand the customer.

Rather than just throwing your net out into the water and hoping there are fish in that spot, now you can go to where the fish are because you know, with absolute certainty, where they are and what they want. The facts have demonstrated it, and it's highly likely that these people will be receptive to your message, as well.

So go to them with something they'll love. By "love," I mean something that ties together everything you've learned about them.

What might they love? Well, what might they find useful? It could be a new type of product or service. It might be a new piece of information or entertainment—and yes, I do see entertainment as useful. It alleviates boredom in a way that delights people. Don't underestimate the power of something like that in people's lives.

If you go with this approach, playing the role of helpful provider, you're removing the guesswork out of trying to create something people will like—especially because you have the data to back it up.

Listening brands create efficiency and accuracy: accuracy because you've learned so much about them that it would be unusual for a consumer not to like what you're offering, and efficiency because you're only going after an audience supported by statistical, data-driven facts.

What happens next, after you provide something to the audience? Then you can measure to see how well it's working. Again, you look for patterns that you see in your communications with them. What messages have they liked? What have they clicked? What did they say in response to what you did, if anything? If not, why didn't they? Where did they go?

As you may be starting to see, this is an iterative process: a constant back-and-forth. Sometimes people are talking to you directly, but sometimes the dialogue is seen just through their movements. It's all data. They're sending signals to you that you can use to create an effective campaign. And you can use data after a campaign, as well.

Or perhaps better still, you could decide never to do a campaign again and focus on having a meaningful dialogue with consumers, instead. Many of the up-and-coming unicorn-like companies follow this type of marketing activity—always on and ready to have a conversation. Of course, to have a meaningful dialogue you will need something to talk about. Data helps there, too, by letting you know the topics your customers are interested in.

A Different Kind of Team

This new strategy has an enormous effect on how a company or agency structures its teams. These teams need to be empowered, first of all. They also need to be comprised of social marketers and data scientists, with the latter, in particular, becoming extremely important today.

It's interesting to think about the way the role of the social marketer has changed. Looking at where a social marketer was working, say, 20 years ago, they probably were engaged in areas like direct marketing, customer service or PR.

The data scientist back then most likely would have been doing the traditional kind of market research that we've been talking about, too.

And in leadership roles, today the head of customer research and the head of customer service are often blended into one person: the chief marketing officer (CMO). We've discussed a bit about the role of today's CMO, but it's an important point to mention in this chapter on teams.

The CMO's job description is dynamically different from what it was 20 years ago. In the old days, the CMO would sit in a high-level meeting and would be viewed—sorry to say—as the person at the table who was wasting the company's money. The sentiment around marketing was, "Sure, go make TV commercials and print ads that may or may not help our sales. We know we have to do these things, but we also know that it's going to end up costing us a lot more money than it's going to bring in." The main reason for that sentiment was that it used to be very difficult to measure the return on investment in marketing.

It's a different game today. Now, the CMO's results are measurable. Their teams can be held accountable. If you're bringing together the qualities of consumer research, customer service and marketing, you're creating an extremely important role within an organization: a role that could be listed in importance just behind the CEO and CFO.

The work of the CMO is not as a "cost center" any longer. It's actually a revenue generator because of our ability to spot opportunities and optimize the use of data. Think about this: Today, every digital interaction with a brand can be the place to buy, as well—"click here to purchase"—whereas in the far past, an ad was only a gentle nudge to consider the brand, nowhere near the point of sale, itself.

It would be difficult to overstate how enormous this switch is in terms of leadership and team building.

With our agency's clients right now, we can see that some organizations have made the switch, but many have not. And the difference to us in working with those organizations is like night and day. The old-school marketer is obsessed with videos and developing the best TV commercial—they talk a lot about "big ideas." They're preoccupied with winning a Cannes Lion, which is our industry's top award. They are also obsessed with finding the perfect combination of imagery and copywriting to express their brand identity. When it comes to objectives and KPIs, they fixate on GRPs (gross rating points—a means for potential audience measurement).

I hate to break it to them, but this is not the future of advertising. It's barely the present tense. Even looking at the awards circuit, it seems to be the more helpful and data-based work that is winning all the accolades. And with regards to Cannes, in 2015 the event organizers started a significant innovation program, which explores new digital and data technologies. In my humble opinion, the speakers and booths were a lot more helpful than anything I heard on the traditional main stage—and the companies in that room are the ones with promising futures.

The Savvy CMO

The savvy CMOs are an entirely different breed. Their obsessions relate to deeply understanding the consumer through data. They want to know everything the consumer likes. They want to be useful and create content that the consumer values, loves and wants to share with other people. They are not precious about who creates the content as long as the consumer and brand benefit from it.

In short, they want to do whatever they have to do in order to be useful and build a connection with people. If they have a hypothesis about the consumer and the data tells them something different, then they're willing to change. They listen to the data, and they respect it, whereas the traditional CMOs continue to trust their intuition because, they believe, it's worked well for them for so many years.

Some CMOs are intimidated by the data, I'm sure. But instead of challenging themselves to learn and grow, they have hunkered down and decided to ignore the way things are going.

They won't have their jobs for long. It's already too late. It's either catch up, or go to work for a staid company that doesn't care about significant growth.

No Such Thing As Average

In all fairness, it's easy to see how marketers could be confused about what to do with all this new data. It used to be that a client would have one big audience they wanted to target, or they'd want to find commonalities between different, slightly smaller audiences. Then those commonalities would be summed up in some sort of campaign, and the campaign would be built around some big, broad theme.

We did all of that because we didn't have effective ways to target people. If you were handing out newspapers, for example, you couldn't give some people a paper with one version of your ad, and another group of people a paper with a different version. In the old days, we were "averaging out" of consumers. It was necessary. It was efficient. And there just wasn't the ability to be so bespoke.

Think about television commercials. It's the same thing. You have to serve everyone the same TV ad at the same time. For the most part, you can't "hyper target" and send one commercial to one household group, and another ad to a different set of households, and withhold the ad altogether from another group. People are either watching the show, or they're not.

Does this concept of "averaging out" even need to exist anymore?

The answer is a resounding, "No." That's a huge shift for both companies and consumers, and I believe it's a wholly positive one.

Because what data can help you do is create micro communities—little buckets of consumers. Let's talk about our dog lovers again. There might be a group of people who love dogs, and they enjoy going hiking, too. We might have another group of people who love their dogs, but it's because they're home alone and the dog provides companionship. Young families, of course, might view their dog as a friend but also as entertainment for their kids.

When you start noticing these segments and sub-segments, you can begin to see them as cultures, in and of themselves. What is the benefit? If your organization is large, you can form micro teams dedicated to each segment and sub-segment.

Now, we can begin seeing organizations in an entirely new way: as having teams devoted to consumers, not teams devoted to products.

Segue to Segments

I've just introduced two concepts that encapsulate a lot of what we've been talking about in this book. In addition to the megaphone changing hands—from company to consumer— we now have the company seeing people for who they really are. They're no longer some vague "average" person, where the company or agency is guessing at what will positively persuade a demographic based on self-reported market research results.

The company is also moving its focus away from questions like, "What product might meet the market need?' and moving toward questions like, "What are people saying, exactly? What are they doing? What are they seeing, reading, watching, listening to every day?" With the technology that's now available to us, we can hear the answers to those questions—and a thousand others we wouldn't have thought to ask—by looking at factual data, recording through people's actions in the digital space.

Let's talk through an example of how segmenting people might work within this new data-driven framework.

You are a car company. Traditionally, you've been set up with your employees grouped into teams based on each automobile model you manufacture and sell. This team over here takes care of the sports car. That one over there, the minivan. And the one in the corner, the truck.

Then, you might say that the sports car is for young people, specifically for young males. The minivan? For stay-at-home moms. And the truck, for working dads.

But what happens when we start listening to the data and we find that stay-at-home moms actually like to drive sports cars and trucks because it makes them feel a sense of freedom and empowerment from their obligations and stressful lives?

What happens is that your car company needs to shift gears.

Instead of grouping teams around products, you group them around consumers. Your baseline question becomes, "How can our team focus more on a specific group of consumers and how we can meet their needs, and less on our products and how we can talk about them?"

I can hear you now.

"But JR, we do put our customers at the center of what we do!"

To which I would ask, do you really?

A company may think it's putting the customer at the center, but if they look closely at what they're actually doing, they're putting the product at the center. Their teams are focused on products, so their teams are built around business units and categories. Rarely—even though it's what I'm suggesting in this book—are companies forming teams around audiences.

But I truly believe that if teams were actually focused on audiences and mini-audiences, they would find themselves building much deeper relationships with their consumers: consumers who would become much more loyal to the brand.

Remembering back to the 1980s and '90s, the idea that a station wagon (big estates or tourers if you're in Europe) was used by families was totally fabricated by ad agency messaging: "It has room, it's easy to get in and out of, and your whole family can fit!" There was no reason at all that companies couldn't have found a way to make station wagons cool to young people. They could have just as easily said, "This station wagon is great for you and all your friends. You can carry your gym kit, skateboard, surfboard, you name it. If there's nowhere for you to hang out, you can throw a party inside your station wagon!"

Clearly I'm exaggerating a bit, but you get the idea.

Even today—and it's really a big reason for my writing this book—companies focus so much on products, messaging and categories that they're totally missing the point: they need to organize themselves around cultures, consumer groups and audiences. They then need to approach marketing from that angle, and a whole lot less from, "What do we want to say?"

Their thinking should first be, "What do we need to understand?"

Think back to Red Bull. What do they focus on? Do they keep playing with their drink product and talking about the taste in new ways, or do they keep finding ways to stay relevant to their audience through content? They lean more heavily on building a relationship with their audience.

In the next chapter, we'll look at a couple of extended examples that will illustrate just how much this shift in thinking can influence a marketing strategy and, ultimately, a company's bottom line.

What You Heard in This Chapter

- Listening brands create efficiency and accuracy, which leads to a greater percentage of offerings that consumers are likely to value.

- With the data available to us now, it's easier to see audiences within audiences, almost like micro-communities and micro-cultures.

- Marketing teams should be organized around these audiences and consumer cultures, instead of around the company's products or services.

Try This

What is an example of a company—other than Red Bull—that you can clearly see is organized around listening to, and responding to, micro-communities of consumers instead of around its own products? What evidence leads you to this conclusion?

LESSONS FROM REAL BRANDS

I thought it might be interesting for you to see firsthand the kinds of questions a digital agency might ask about a client's company from this listening point of view.

How Can We Help "FreshDent"?

Remember my example earlier about "FreshDent," the mint and candy company? Well as I'm typing this chapter, I'm also working on a brief addressing a very similar challenge. The goal of the brief is to answer this question: How do we make breath mints relevant to young people, on a global scale?

Young people have stopped consuming mints and candy—or at least, they consume a whole lot less of it than they used to. As I'm writing a response to this brief, and I keep thinking that we're missing what it's going to take to change their behavior. We can't simply go to these young people with a message through the megaphone: "Our mint is cool! Our mint is fresh! Our mint lasts a long time! Our mint tastes good and will attract the opposite sex!"

That's old-school marketing thinking, where the brand is holding the megaphone and the young people are eagerly waiting for any message we shout at them. Magically, they'll run to the corner shop and buy FreshDent candy mints.

Not. Going. To. Happen.

So what should we do? That's actually not a rhetorical question. Think about all we've talked about so far, and see if what I'm about to say meshes with what you would do if you were the marketing group for FreshDent.

First, we need to organize ourselves in such a way that we can deeply understand young people, so we know what matters to them, what's on their mind, what they're doing. We need to find a way to play a role in what they're already doing—to become relevant, to stay relevant and, most importantly, to be useful to them.

The only way we're going to be able to do that is if we stop obsessing over, "We have mints and we need to sell mints!"

Instead, we need to think like this: "We have an audience. We need to get close to them. We need to become good friends with them."

As of right now, I'd recommend to this client that they build a team made largely of young people or hire up some young consultants. This team should be commissioned with the task of understanding, relating to and building rapport with other young people and, ultimately, develop something that is useful to them, as well as look closely at the digital and social data from young people in their most important markets.

Where might they start?

All young people—yesterday, today and tomorrow—need a sense of self, a sense of identity. They're going through a crucial development stage in life, and they're trying to prepare themselves to leave home. It's a physical stage and a psychological stage: a period of tremendous psychological growth, when they start to want independence and they start to create that independence in their lives. While doing all of this, they're trying to sort out who they are and what makes them unique.

The most important thing you can give a young person is a sense of identity, which is related to their self-esteem. In the 1950s, chewing gum (and sadly, cigarettes) was a way to look cool. Gum somehow captured the essence of swagger.

But that's been lost now. Candy, mints and gum do not play that role. Today, the thing that helps young people look and feel cool and interesting, that gives them that sense of swagger, is social media. It's all about, "Did a lot of people like my picture? Was it shared? Do people like my Snapchat stories? Do a lot of people follow me?" Literally, it's all about this: "Do I have other people's attention in the form of followers, clicks, likes?" A person's social media footprint speaks to their social credentials.

So how can FreshDent, as a brand that cares about young people, help them get more attention on social media? How can we help raise their self-esteem? And how can we do this from the standpoint of a brand that just so happens to also sell breath mints?

We need to find ways to associate ourselves with the improvement of their self-esteem and the raising of their cool factor.

As I finish writing this section, we are still working on making FreshDent a relevant brand. But because you've read this far in the book, you know exactly where we'll start to look for answers to the "how" questions. We'll listen to young people via scouring the data produced by their movements online, and from there, we'll have our answer as to how to be helpful to them.

Learning from Red Bull

I also want to talk more about Red Bull, because this is such an interesting brand. Originally invented and sold in Thailand, Red Bull has been around since 1987. If you've never tasted it, I would recommend caution. It's actually quite a potent-tasting drink: an acquired taste as they say, and it has a lot of caffeine in it.

But this drink has become so important to culture—really

the world culture—today because of its intelligent marketing. They really understand their audience, first and foremost.

Red Bull has been able to build an intensely personal relationship with its audience through the things these people care about. The fact that Red Bull serves up a weird-flavored, highly caffeinated drink almost has nothing to do with the relationship it has created with is audience, because people don't drink Red Bull for the taste, (At least, I hope they don't.) People drink it because they think it's cool. Sure, it gives them a little bit of energy, but largely it's because Red Bull is associated with being cool.

So how has Red Bull been able to do this? It's because they've moved into areas that are of high resonance with the people they're trying to reach. They have Red Bull studios that are producing music and film that young people just love, so they're meeting an entertainment need. It's not like they're just running a ton of TV, banner or print ads. They doing things for, and giving things to, young people, and it's all helping to build their reputation with this audience.

Red Bull hosts events: parties, races and other fun events. In doing so, they're being helpful because they're alleviating boredom and giving young people a way to connect, a way to hang out together. Again, all of this activity has very little to do with the beverage category. It doesn't address whether it tastes good, or if it's nutritional, and so forth. But Red Bull is popular because they deeply understand how to relate to their consumer in a useful way.

Most importantly, they have moved away from what so many

other brands do, which is to yell, promote, push and shove their messaging onto people.

For some companies, this handing over of the megaphone—well, it's actually been yanked from them—may give them a sense of losing control of their brand. The truth is, if companies don't embrace this new consumer-centered way of building their brand, they will have even less control.

All it takes is one negative tweet. One bad review that goes viral. One scathing comment.

If they can simply learn to listen more often than they speak, they're actually creating more control of the brand. They may want to ignore this new paradigm, but retaining control of their image is just an illusion. The stage doesn't belong to them now, and social media is responsible for this major marketing shift.

Start Now, Start Small

My best piece of advice: start now. Do something small. It's not necessary to fire the old teams and hire new ones. See how people can begin to be retrained or reorganized. Perhaps you just do business as usual, but on the side you set up a small team to experiment with this sort of thinking: a startup within your own company.

One way to look at this is with the concept of A/B testing. With A/B testing, you put two versions of the same message, for example, out into the digital space with one variable changed. Whichever one gets the most clicks, views, shares—whatever single variable you're testing—is the one that wins.

You could think about using that same formula inside a company. Keep one team as it always has been. Set up a second that has a mandate to try this new approach. Then, see which one generates better results. And these two teams can learn from one another. Experiment. Have fun. Play.

The idea that marketing structures are the same as they were even three years ago? Not true. The degree of collaboration you need among team members is much higher. So start experimenting in a small way, and see what happens.

If you're looking for ways to continually refine your offering, data can provide significant answers to questions about what's working and what isn't. That's what we'll cover in the next chapter.

What You Heard in This Chapter

- Start moving away from the idea of "we have a product to sell" and toward "we have an audience we need to deeply understand and deliver value to."

- A company that focuses on its consumers' culture and actually builds a culture within that—like Red Bull does—is an example of a listening brand.

- Start small by doing A/B testing with digital messaging and/or with teams within a company, with one team doing the marketing status quo and the other being more listening-centric.

Try This

What's an example of a company that's similar to Red Bull, which has integrated itself seamlessly into its audience's culture to the point where its product or service is almost secondary?

CHAPTER 13

HOW DATA CAN BE USED TO REFINE MESSAGE, PRODUCT AND CONTEXT

The campaign-centric model of marketing is over. At least, if you want to be a company that remains viable—and visible—in the minds of consumers, it is.

The Tent Pole Effect

Imagine you're looking at an annual marketing calendar as a line graph. With this new paradigm we've been talking about, you would see continual back-and-forth communication with consumers, with the occasional "tent pole" popping up: any big initiative, new product launch or new service that you need to break out above the rest.

You never stop communicating, and you never stop listening. But there will be those moments when you need to talk a bit more.

With the traditional campaign-centric model, companies would take a lot of time to be inward focused and prepare everything. Then they would launch this campaign—with an overarching theme based on the outdated "brand model" I talked about early in the book—and the campaign might last for a number of weeks, depending on how much money they had to spend on it.

Then they would just go absolutely quiet until the next campaign. Crickets.

To be fair, it wasn't just marketing that suffered from this strategy. Companies did this with everything—like product development. A company would focus on innovating one or two products and spend a lot of time researching those products. Then, of course, they would launch those products.

Sound familiar?

But if we can learn from some of the digital companies out there—like Google, Facebook or Twitter—we can see that they're constantly listening to consumers and adjusting their products and services depending on what the consumers like and what the consumers want. It's a continual process.

You never stop communicating. You definitely never stop listening.

Quick example: Gmail. With Google's mail service, people

had been saying that they wished there were a button to retrieve an email they had sent. You can imagine times when you've sent an email, and maybe you wished you hadn't. Gmail didn't have this kind of button before, but now it does because they listened to what people were saying they wanted.

This example might not seem all that groundbreaking, but it illustrates a key point here. I seriously doubt that the Google team had tons of meetings about how they could develop and release a new feature on their email service. They probably just got enough people saying that they wished they could do that, and someone at Google said, "Yeah, why don't we just build it?"

Not too long after this, Facebook has also decided to roll out their version of a "dislike" button. Facebook Reactions will allow users to express more than one type of emotion through additional buttons under posts. They listened to what the people wanted. We've all seen pictures and news stories of injustice on Facebook, and if you want to acknowledge this, than a "like" button feels kind of wrong. Both Facebook and Gmail changed their platforms as a direct response to customer needs. You may think this is easier with digital-based products, and you may be right, but at least be open to learning from digital. Nike did when they invented their Nike ID program so that now you can customize almost any of their shoe models.

If we move away from campaign-based thinking toward always having a dialogue with consumers, then it means we have to be ready when a conversation starts to kick off or circle around something new, like a product or service. Following my advice about creating segments and sub-segments of customers to pay attention to, your teams will notice when topics keep coming up. Things will start to scale in the consumers' conversations.

A company needs to hear those things, of course, but secondly, it needs to be able to respond. If it's an "unsend" button on their email service or a product line change, then those people within the company who are listening need to be able to take action. They have to be respected enough to be allowed to do so.

This is where marketing team members start to be viewed as more like customer service experts and drivers of new research and development than simply marketers, because they form the center of consumer insights. They're now on the front lines of understanding what consumers want. Through data, they can prove that there is significant interest in a new product or service.

What's really amazing is how this all comes full circle. Their way of demonstrating that the company cares about consumers it that they make things happen that consumers want. This is key: they actually have to deliver on change for the consumers.

What "Responsive" Marketing Really Means

I'd like to show you something else that has shifted rather dramatically in this 24-hour digital world we live in.

The prevalent idea about branding is that a "company" is a functional thing—offering products and/or services—but a brand is an added layer of personality or tone: something intangible that creates an emotional connection with the consumer. You can have two products there are exactly the same, but if one has a good brand around it, then it suddenly has more value to the consumer.

The challenge is that simply communicating tone or personality is not enough anymore, because today's consumers are too smart for that. They've grown up in these extremely branded worlds. And teen-agers and 20-somethings are branding themselves on YouTube, Instagram, Snapchat—you name it. These young people are even using the term "brand" to describe themselves because people today really understand the power of a brand.

Now for companies and organizations to brand themselves, they have to go beyond having a tone or personality and just being consistent in portraying it. The way to build a connection with these extremely brand-savvy people is that they have to go above and beyond.

They have to provide new and relevant services.

They have to get into deep conversations with consumers.

They have to create experiences with people.

You can't just project an image and attitude anymore, because people will see through it. The know it's just fluff and marketing mumbo-jumbo.

You have to listen, respond and then meet their unmet needs.

This new way of brand building doesn't happen just by creating new products and services in response to what you're hearing, either.

For instance, maybe people can't find your customer service number, so they reach out via social media—and you have to respond quickly. Maybe a lot of people don't understand a certain feature of a product, so you have to chat with them in a personable, direct way. Maybe they think your car is cool but they don't know how to put a baby's car seat in it, so you create a video to show them.

The needs of consumers are infinite. But now it's a marketing person's job to understand those needs, and they have to be able to respond and act. Listening allows companies big and small to infinitely personalize their responses and relationships to customers, by meeting them where they are and by anticipating their needs. They can surprise and delight customers, and they create value through extraordinary company-to-consumer experiences, not through branding.

From Sappy to Snappy

Here's a great example of a successful company tweaking its message, product and context based on data they picked up from listening in this way.

Bodyform is a feminine hygiene product company. In the past, they had always branded themselves in the traditional way: campaigns filled with images of women running on the beach with the wind blowing through hair, that sort of thing.

The message was always along the lines of, "Everything is great. Life is wonderful, so get out there and enjoy it. With Bodyform, you can do whatever you want without worry."

Honestly, it was a little over the top and sappy.

Then one day in 2012, a man wrote to Bodyform on Facebook. A clever, cheeky Brit, he composed a jovial essay of a post telling Bodyform, "You lied!" He went on to say that Bodyform said that when his wife was having her period, everything was going to be fine. She would be herself— same as always—and life would be pleasant, wonderful and beautiful, complete with her running on the beach and horseback riding.

His post was hilarious on purpose, and his main message was pretty simple: Bodyform's ads and commercials are obviously not based on reality, certainly not the reality of the women in his life. As you might imagine, this post went viral—it got a lot of traction in social media.

Bodyform responded brilliantly. At the time, they had an agency that was paying very close attention to what was happening in social media around the brand. In that moment, they realized the tone the company had had for its brand was completely wrong. It was an outdated way of talking about themselves. This man—being funny and cheeky about his wife's period—was getting more traction than any of their traditional brand communications.

In literally a two-day turnaround, the agency and Body-form decided they were going to make a film in answer to this man's post. In the film, the supposed CEO of Bodyform responds in cheeky kind. She admits that they have, indeed, lied to the public: that a woman's period is actually not a wonderful time of the month, and things are not always cheery, perfect and pleasant. Mind you, this was all said in a very humorous way.

But she was, in fact, apologizing to this man for misleading him—and the British public. The reason, she said, was that they didn't feel the public could handle the truth of what really happens each month. To add to the effect, the CEO's message had some imagery of men sitting in focus groups watching the reality (that part was off screen!). Their faces showed fear and mortification.

It was tongue in cheek, but it was real, at the same time. And it came across very, very well. It won awards because Bodyform was one of the first companies to respond to a consumer in this way.

For me, it was a big insight that a brand can talk about itself for years a certain way, and overnight it can change. Just one well-connected person in social media can disrupt a brand, flip it on its head, turn it around and throw it off message.

And if Bodyform hadn't been listening and hadn't responded? They would have become sort of a joke, I think. The man's post would have gained more and more traction. If they had not been listening, they also would have missed the opportunity to do a cool project, which in return won them a prestigious Cannes Lions award.

Social media is a reflection of the world. It's hard to know exactly how this process happens, but let's say Bodyform had continued down its traditional path. Women who used the product might have been tempted to switch because the brand itself begins to look weak—which, of course, makes it vulnerable to competitors.

What else can we learn from this example? We can listen more effectively than our competitors do. By listening and responding, by joining in the conversation in a helpful way, we can begin to draw even the most loyal consumers away from brands they have supported for decades. This is happening every day.

Once a company loses its emotional appeal and it isn't focused on building rapport with consumers, it becomes commoditized. Then, you start reducing margins and looking for ways to save. And before long, the company is slowly dying. If you don't respond to consumers and someone else does, they'll start asking themselves, "Hey, why am I buying this brand again? They're not even listening to me."

Responsive Technology

It's not just teams of people doing this listening, of course. There's another entity involved in this process.

Let's say I search for a GE microwave because I've always

bought GE. It never crosses my mind to buy another brand of small appliance. So I'm on Google, and a little ad pops up at the top of the page telling me about a Samsung microwave.

Within less than a second, because of cookies and all the other data connections—IDs and numbers I'm generating online—I'm served up this ad for Samsung. And not only that, but I see something in the Samsung ad related to the gym, which I go to frequently: "The gym's a lot easier when you spend less time cooking."

All within less than a second!

The algorithms are so sophisticated, it's like they "knew" me. Now, something has happened in my mind, where even though I've had so many years of loyalty to GE, in that moment I might think, "I never even thought about looking at Samsung. And I have to go to the gym today. I don't want to forget."

All of this was built into one ad because the algorithms could see what other websites I had been to. This is an everyday, but amazing, use of data. Just recently, I spoke to a company that has created a system to develop ads that are so customized, only a few people will end up seeing the exact same message. This is happening more and more, and it's truly mind-blowing.

So even if it's not other humans sitting at a desk somewhere and listening, it's computers and systems within computer software.

Can you imagine the kind of impact this will have? It will have a huge impact—at least for a short while. Then in time, just like we're all very accustomed to brands and branding and see straight through it, we'll see straight through those customized ads, too.

The Revolution Has Just Begun

We're still at the beginning of a revolution within communications, where every single person can have bespoke responses and bespoke ads to sent them. We're even working on the technology now so that if you are walking down a street with your mobile phone, your mobile phone can talk to a digital billboard, a bus stop sign or even an image on the side of a building. It can say, "Oh! Here comes JR. He has been looking at this product a lot recently. We should serve him an ad right now while he's walking by the billboard."

So I'll see it, and a new awareness is created in my mind. Then whoever is next behind me in line or on the sidewalk— well, their phone sends a new signal, and the ad is bespoke to them. We've seen this in the movies, but it's actually possible now.

With all this talk of what's happening today and what's going to be happening in the future, I'd like to pause for a moment to reflect on why people loved—still love—the old way of doing things.

It was fun!

You could talk to your family and friends and say, "My commercial is on TV," or "Look, my ads are in these magazines." There's something really cool about going to a photo shoot or working on a storyboard for a car commercial and then going on location with a famous director and celebrity. That's glamorous. Marketing was the fun part of business.

On the industry circuit, there are always awards for best ad campaign and so forth. The traditional advertising world is a well-oiled machine.

At the time of this writing, however, the UK will be the first market in which 50 percent of the advertising spend will be done in digital spaces. This is a huge shift, because that means that from this year onward, the majority of advertising in the UK will be digital, and a lot of digital advertising is automatically adapted for the unique viewer.

When you start to see these non-digital spaces try to catch up, it's almost like they're thinking along the lines of, "How can we use data to make our service better?" Then you see things like newspapers' websites being able to tell the news company more about their readership by using the data. In doing so, they could begin, let's say, to have different versions of newspapers delivered to different homes. The offline world is often trying its best to behave like the digital world.

This can definitely happen in print media. We're already using data to figure out where to put posters and billboards, for example, because we can use mobile IDs and GPS targeting to see what type of people walk on which streets.

The Final Frontiers?

In my view, the last big switch will be in television. It will become programmatic. By that I mean, just like when you go to YouTube and search for videos on your computer, you'll see things that I don't see because the data signals are serving you ads that they "think"—algorithmically speaking—will resonate with you.

Not too long from now, our TVs will be so digitally connected that they'll do the same thing. I'll be watching CNN news, and you'll be watching CNN news, even at the same time—but when the ad break happens, I'll be served a different set of ads that relate to me, and vice versa.

Let's fly way, way up into the sky for a bird's eye view about what this means for society. It means that people are going to be living very different experiences even though they may be right beside each other. People are going to believe that they're operating in a world that's like them, even though another person will feel the same way, but their world—their culture—is entirely different. If every time you go on a computer or on your phone, every time you watch TV, every time you walk by a digital billboard, every time you get your newspaper enhanced by data: it's all catering to the things you like. But you won't even be seeing the things that I see during my day.

In the next chapter, we'll come back down to Earth for another look at how any, and every, business can become more digitally savvy.

What You Heard in This Chapter

▣ Listening allows companies—both big and small—to
infinitely personalize their responses and relationships
to customers by meeting them where they are and by
anticipating their needs.

▣ Companies paying attention to data are more able to surprise and delight customers and create value through
extraordinary company-to-consumer experiences—not
through branding.

▣ Technology is changing so fast and is become so much
smarter, it will become easier to have a much more per-
sonalized experience as a consumer.

Try This

Next time you're online, start watching for how often you're
having a customized experience based on your web-surfing
habits. It may be difficult for you to spot, because this type of
experience is becoming more commonplace. What trends
do you notice? Which companies seem to be most obviously
listening to data in your personal online world?

CHAPTER 14

HOW TO AVOID BEING A DINOSAUR

Listening to and responding to customers isn't a new idea. Companies have been doing that for centuries. What's new is that we can do this listening at deeper levels—and so much faster and better—because of the digital world that we live in and all the data that's created from it.

Even huge non-digital companies that tend to move slowly can be responsive. Even the gigantic Coca-Cola is responding to people's concerns about their food and healthy eating and living, especially in the US. Now the company actually has more products that are at least not as harmful for you, than products that are controversial.

But it is a lot easier for companies that are wholly represented in the digital space, such as Airbnb and Netflix, to respond faster and more effectively.

We also have companies like the behemoth Amazon which, because of its infrastructure built for listening—having so many people interacting on a smooth, wonderfully optimized digital experience—is able to grow to such a scale that it could easily buy one of the traditional store chains in the United States as a delivery location. Companies that have been built in the digital space have grown to such an extent that they're now a clear threat to brick-and-mortar companies. Hugely successful companies in the digital space, like Apple, Amazon and Google, could enter into any category they want to now—and probably improve upon that category—because they know their consumers better than anyone else.

For instance, if Google really wants to go into the automotive industry, it has enough cash on hand that it could buy one of the traditional automotive companies. They could create a seamless digital experience so that the car would be completely connected to the lifestyles the drivers are accustomed to.

This type of thing isn't that far away. Keep watching and keep listening for these business trends. Because these types of companies started with an infrastructure in place that was trying to be more useful, more helpful—one that was listening for opportunities more than it was trying to find a way to simply sell and push what was on the shelves.

Let's spend a few more sentences on Airbnb, because it's a great example of a listening brand's advantage over another brand that hasn't joined in the conversation.

Airbnb is an amazing story of two gentlemen who were designers. They were planning to attend a professional conference, but they couldn't afford to go to the conference and pay for a hotel. From that rather typical experience, they had an insight. The company started by the two of them renting inflatable air mattresses and serving breakfast in their San Francisco apartment to help pay the rent—thus, "air bed & breakfast."

Today, you have major brands doing everything they can to partner with and be relevant to Airbnb. You have hotel chains suffering because most likely, they didn't listen for the trends soon enough or weren't responding to the trends quickly enough to meet the needs of a huge group of people who were priced out of travel. And not just priced out, but they also might have wanted a more authentic travel experience.

If a company like Hilton or Marriott had been listening to data, it would have had better insights into what types of services people wanted, like local tour guides, event recommendations or something customized to the rooms that make people feel more welcome. Perhaps they needed different tiers in the pricing so that everyone from young people with lower incomes all the way up to high-income people could experience the same hotel. At the very least, they needed a social media program in place that was leveraging the experiences people had in their hotels and hotel rooms. Hilton could have taken advantage of people's reviews, guests' stories and pictures above one-way corporate communications. But they didn't do that soon enough, and Airbnb, with their great social strategies, dominated people's feeds with peer recommendations. Today, most people in the west are well aware of Airbnb, which is now on the shortlist when people are considering places to stay. And Airbnb is still leveraging the voice of the people. When you visit their site, you see that the experience is centered wholly on the voice of the people: through their unique descriptions of their homes and properties, or through the reviews of others. Airbnb, as a corporate entity, has very little to say.

In short, a Hilton or a Marriott could have made itself as irresistible to travelers as Airbnb if—big "if"—it had been able to capture insights through listening to data on the scale we've been talking about.

It's hard to know what a company like Hilton will do next, but I'm betting they are looking at ways to change their business model to be more responsive.

Start with Social and Search Data

Wherever you are right now in your ability to listen to data with technology and your teams, just start. And start with social listening, because it's the easiest way for you to see what people are saying about your brand online through hashtags and such. If two or more people are saying the same thing, it's a pretty sure bet that many people are thinking it.

When you see something start to scale, you can be certain that those people represent a much larger group of people's internal monologue.

What's great about starting with social data is that it allows you to combat anything negative about your brand before it can affect the bottom line. In fact, you may find that by listening, you'll actually learn what *has* been affecting the bottom line—a reason that might have been invisible to you up to this point. Having social listening in place will give you a sense of the exact reason your company isn't working well for people anymore.

Search can also tell you quite a bit about what people are looking for, and you can begin to respond. One thing that's become clear to me from reviewing so much search data is that good customer service practices are a must. It's more important than most companies realize today. If people are searching for your product, and if the other word they're using has any type of emotion associated with it, you can see exactly how people think about your product.

There is a lot of "how to" out there in searching behaviors, as well: many people type in that phrase as an inquiry. For example, if someone types "How to fix my broken Samsung" into the search box, that already starts to tell Samsung that its product is failing people and the content that the company will need to create as a response.

Once you decide to go further into data analysis, you'll need an agency to help. If a company is running any type of advertisements, promoted posts or paid ads around search, the agency or the platform placing those ads should be providing reports to help you understand the results and—more importantly—the implications of the results. These reports can show how the ads performed as well as aggregated information about the consumers who engaged with the ads: where else they were looking, their demographics and so forth.

Here's the important thing: Once a company decides to start playing in this digital space, the digital space will respond with insights. It's the give-and-take of doing business in this digital ecosystem we're all a part of now.

Dinosaurs and Unicorns

If there's any concern over whether it's too late for you to begin, I'd like to address that fear by talking about dinosaurs and unicorns.

A unicorn is a digital-based business that gets valued at an extremely high amount very quickly, such as Snapchat, WhatsApp or Instagram. Their whole business model is that they have a lot of upfront investment to help them get really big before the company starts to make a significant return. They're called unicorns because they start being valued at rather crazy numbers—like $3 billion!—before they've even made any profit. It's a bit fantastical, to say the least.

But these types of companies are still being created every day. Snapchat, for example, wasn't even relevant two years ago. Now, it's enormous. If I think about myself, am I expert at getting insights, intelligence and data from Snapchat? No, not yet. But I'm going to have to figure it out, just as any marketer will who is joining the game today. We're learning about Snapchat at the same time.

So every time a new unicorn enters the equation, we all have to start again. It's an even playing field, so stepping onto the field at any point in time is better than staying on the sidelines.

A dinosaur company is one that is not digital savvy and is not listening: the companies that are doing business like they've always done and, to be blunt, these companies are probably going to be destroyed by a unicorn. Big taxi companies are a good example, because as of this writing, they're under destruction by Uber.

And if you think you're in a sector that's immune, think again. Even something as basic as Procter and Gamble's Gillette razors have shown that they're not immune. We can go into every drugstore in the world, probably, and there will be Gillette razors.

How could a unicorn company possibly disrupt that?

Well, now you have the Dollar Shave Club, which is an online membership that sends razors to its subscribers on a monthly basis. You never have to go to a store to buy razors ever again. It's an efficient business model because they know exactly how many razors they need to produce based on the number of subscribers they have. The brand has become a social media darling through its funny videos and clever targeting.

Even something as supposedly stable as beer sales by the big companies are being threatened by breweries that are mailing beer directly to consumers. We could see soda being threatened by companies that finally make a healthy version that's mailed to them monthly. And then suddenly, giant Coca-Cola would be suffering. We almost witnessed people making sodas at home, but both Pepsi and Coke now have partnerships with "do it yourself" soda machine makers.

Every business—every single one—can be revolutionized by these digital-savvy, data listening-centric organizations that are popping up left and right. There's a lot of money to be made, so they're going to come into being faster and faster.

I don't say this to scare you, but to encourage you. Even the big, non-digitally based companies can compete in this new world. For example, Gillette started its own version of a shaving club to stop the quick success of that other online ordering service. If they hadn't been listening inside the social media community, they wouldn't have seen it coming— and they might have been shut out of the online membership market really quickly. They acted fast in response to what they've learned through listening and analyzing data, so my guess is that they probably continue to win offline and online and ultimately win the long game. They're not becoming a dinosaur anytime soon.

The good companies get it, and even if they're not quite there, they're trying. They're listening and changing themselves because the consumers are telling them that they need to change. That megaphone is now in the hands of the consumer, and it's not going back to the status quo anytime soon, if ever.

What You Heard in This Chapter

▧ Listening to your customer in this way allows you to provide services and offerings that consumers want and love, thereby making your company relevant to their lives.

▧ Insights from data analysis can allow you to change course quickly to stay in the game instead of becoming a dinosaur.

▧ The best news is that no one has mastered any of this yet. It's still early, which is good news for you—there's plenty of time to catch up.

Try This

What's another example of a well-established, non-digital brand that has responded quickly by shifting a major part of its business to the digital space, based on consumer demand? How successful have they been, and why?

THE FUTURE OF LISTENING TO DATA

When I imagine the future of listening to data, I think of...

Artificial Intelligence

Yes, AI.

I know it sounds like weird android robots, thanks to Hollywood's portrayal of AI. But it's really algorithms and computers making decisions quickly on their own. As those systems improve, the computer starts to use the data to learn. The rise in programmatic paired with commentary and sentiment analysis will start the momentum. It's still going to be wires, coding, metal and boxes. But believe it or not, this is happening already. AI is a hot topic in the world of advertising and marketing.

We're not talking about doomsday stuff or anything like that. I'll give you an example of how AI is coming up in the advertising and marketing conversation.

When I was in Cannes recently for the Cannes Lions International Festival of Creativity, many people speaking on stage were talking about the shift to artificial intelligence. When a computer can automatically design an ad—choosing the perfect images, predicting the viewers mood, writing a sequence of persuasive words—well, that changes everything, including making certain people less highly valued if they've only been working in the traditional way.

I believe that at some point, a computer will be able to do all of this better than a human can.

You Can Do This

This next comment may sound strange after what I just said about artificial intelligence, but listening to data is nothing to be intimidated by. If you'll remember early on in this book, I explained that I left the traditional world of communication and branding and jumped—that's really how it felt—into the data-obsessed world of digital media. I did it because I knew that it was what I needed to learn because that's the way things were moving.

I also knew that it was learnable. I'd eventually know what I needed to know to be successful in the digital world.

You will, too.

Try not to believe that it's too hard or too intimidating, or that you're too far behind. Maybe if you're close to retirement, you can take that stance. Because anyone middle-aged or younger who works in marketing has to change, adapt and evolve.

Disruptions are happening fast: faster than ever before. Computer systems are getting exponentially faster at learning, too. What took computers two years to do was whittled down to one year, then six months, then a month, then five seconds, and then less than a second.

This progression is having a fallout effect on the world we live in because it allows industries to change faster—and as a result, some businesses, including advertising agencies, can become irrelevant very quickly now.

The main message I'd like to leave you with is this: Please, don't be intimidated. Start learning. Keep learning. Be curious.

If you're already in this digital world, then please stay curious. You're waiting to hear what you don't know—that's the attitude, the way of approaching problems, that you need to adopt.

One reason this method of discovery is so different is because there is some humility to it. You're basically saying, "I don't know," and you're allowing consumers to tell you what you don't know about what they want. So that's the attitude shift.

Key Questions to Ask

In terms of tangible changes, the most important thing to do is to take a serious look at your company's internal practices, including team members. Are they obsessed with making the beautiful Hollywood TV commercials, or are they really curious about how they can better provide a service to the consumers that the company needs to reach? Are you partnered with the right people externally? Does your agency even know what it's doing in terms of digital data? Are they curious about it? Because if they're not, they are the wrong agency for you, and you need to find a new partner with people who are willing to do what it takes to provide you with this information.

Agencies are the ones to help you plan, buy, activate and measure all the digital "stuff," for lack of a better word. They're on the front lines of the data and, consequently, of the insights. The agencies that are very charismatic with good sales people who want to take you to dinner and spend hundreds of dollars on good wine? I'd be very skeptical about those agencies—if they're not also excellent at digital and data. Chances are your future partner is a bit more nerdy than charismatic, or at least they carry a nice balance between the two.

Next question to consider as you go into the future: Do you understand how the big tech players work? I'm talking about the Googles, the Facebooks, the Twitters, the Alibabas, the WeChats, the Yadexes, the Amazons, the Yahoos, the AOLs, plus all the different platforms around the world. Do you have a sense of how they work, and how their experiences work? Because that's what people are engaging in every day. People are spending tons of time in those spaces. If you're going to understand digital, start there. Experiment!

Treat Yourself Like a Consumer

On my phone, for example, I have lots of apps. I don't like some of these apps, but I use them so that I can understand how they work and what the end user's experience is like. I visit a lot of websites every day because I want to understand how they work. I want to see how different people are connecting in the digital world.

I interact with things, I play with things and I look at things as a normal person—with my own unique interests. Even if they have no value to me, personally, as a marketer who needs to understand the people that do like those things, I play with them. I dabble and have fun. I'm in no way whatsoever a techie or engineer. My brain is not even tilted that way.

Personally, I like paper books. I like pictures made with paint. I like walking through the park. I like turning my phone off. I like spending time with dogs. I like talking to my friends around the table with a pint of beer. That is who I am, but I know that if I'm a marketer and my job is to connect my company to millions, if not billions, of people, that not everyone has my same existence and not everyone has my same values. I have to understand other ways of living.

As I learned on the farm growing up, I still need to connect with people wherever they are and with what they love to do.

That's a mistake that many marketers make: they only want to do what they love doing. That's okay, of course, but they're going to need to stay in a position or in a role that may or may not be relevant much longer. If they want to move up in the world of marketing, including becoming a leader in the field, they will need to adjust and do the things I've talked about in this book.

I understand that when we have an innate interest in one thing, and we're intimidated by another, mixing those two together can create a lot of dissonance.

The answer is pretty simple: Enjoy the dissonance. It's the space where creativity lights up...and new ideas emerge.

And you know what's even simpler?

Be curious.

Be helpful.

Be a listening brand.

What You Heard in This Chapter

▣ Artificial intelligence may be the next frontier in terms of data-driven advertising and marketing.

▣ Take a hard look at the people on your teams, both internal and external, and ask if they're really interested in listening to data and using it as the foundation for all of your branding efforts.

- Treat yourself like a consumer and get curious as to how others are experiencing life online.

Try This

Download one of the more popular social media apps to your phone that you don't personally use. What trends do you see, such as people's demographics, topics they're talking about, images they're sharing?

THE AUTHOR

JR LITTLE is a top media professional with over fifteen years experience in marketing and advertising, across multiple sectors with a wide range of Fortune 500 companies. From technology to finance to healthcare to consumer goods, JR has helped to shape and develop the messages and brands of some of the biggest companies in the world, around the world.